A Journey Around The

EAST

MIDLANDS

By Rail In The 1970s and 1980s

A review of mainly BR era operations in the East Midlands, including coverage of the mechanical signalling in the 'Leicester Gap' on the Midland Main Line.

Graham R. Jelly

Sunday 7th May 1978. Ratcliffe-on-Soar: The East Midlands is well represented here. Class 46 46026 THE LEICESTERSHIRE AND DERBYSHIRE YEOMANRY heading the 0851 Leeds to Penzance express is in Nottinghamshire, having been diverted on to the Midland Railway's London line as far as Wigston North Junction in lieu of the unavailable direct route from Derby to Birmingham. East Midlands Parkway station, now on this site, was many years in the future at this time.

(*Front cover picture*) **Friday 28th September 1979. Bottesford West Junction**: The view from Orston Lane level crossing, as Class 31 31284 passes the outlet from the Up goods loop and approaches the junction with empty 100-ton oil tanks from the Total Oil terminal at Colwick, Nottingham to the Lindsey Oil Refinery, Immingham.

(*Rear cover pictures*) **Sunday 11th March 1979. Rufford Colliery**: In the heart of Nottinghamshire this colliery opened in 1928, a year after Clipstone, its near neighbour to the north. The LMSR built a railway serving both, from Rufford Colliery Branch Junction on the former MR Mansfield to Rolleston Junction line. The LNER branched south from Rufford Junction, on the former GCR 'Mansfield Railway' from Clipstone to Kirkby South Junction serving Rufford and later some other collieries, as deeper mines were opened ever further east in the coalfield. This duplication of lines was common and only slowly addressed by BR. Though LMSR, the signal box (seen here looking north) and signals were in the style of the MR. The signal box closed on 29th November 1981, the colliery thereafter being served only from the north until production ended in 1993. Clipstone Colliery survived until 2003. Nevertheless, in 1979 the past lived on - just.

First published in the United Kingdom by
BOOK LAW PUBLICATIONS 2018
382 Carlton Hill, Nottingham, NG4 1JA
Printed and bound by The Amadeus Press, Cleckheaton, West Yorkshire.

A Journey Around The East Midlands By Rail In The 1970s and 1980s

CONTENTS

Tuesday 21st March 1977. Leicester: The 'Leicester Gap' - an oasis of mechanical signalling between the power boxes of Trent and West Hampstead, extending for 55 miles between Loughborough and Sharnbrook, is exemplified by the forest of semaphores controlled by Leicester North, Bell Lane and Humberstone Road Junction signal boxes. This view is from Swain Street bridge, immediately north of Leicester station. Class 45 45123 THE LANCASHIRE FUSILIER arrives with the 1510 from Nottingham to London (St Pancras) while, meanwhile a Class 08 shunter is busy in the yard.

THE EAST MIDLANDS

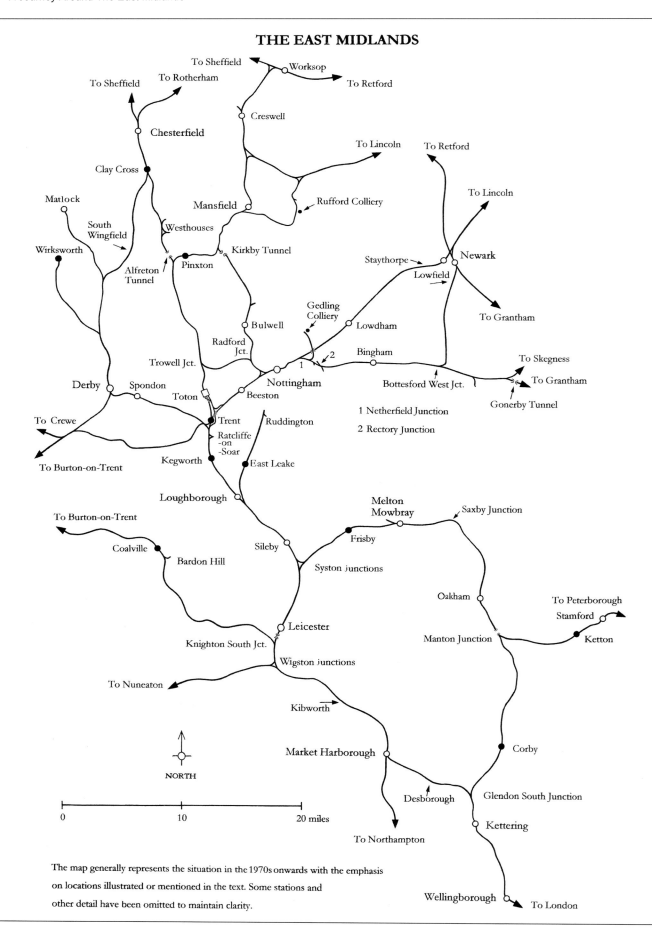

To Sheffield
Worksop
To Retford
To Rotherham
To Sheffield
Creswell
Chesterfield
To Lincoln
To Retford
Clay Cross
To Lincoln
Matlock
Mansfield
Rufford Colliery
Newark
South Wingfield
Westhouses
Staythorpe
Lowfield
Wirksworth
Kirkby Tunnel
Alfreton Tunnel
Pinxton
Gedling Colliery
Bulwell
Lowdham
Radford Jct.
2
Bingham
To Skegness
Trowell Jct.
1
To Grantham
Nottingham
Bottesford West Jct.
Derby   Spondon
Toton   Beeston
Gonerby Tunnel
To Crewe
Trent
Ruddington
1 Netherfield Junction
Ratcliffe -on -Soar
2 Rectory Junction
Kegworth   East Leake
To Burton-on-Trent
Loughborough
Melton Mowbray
Saxby Junction
To Burton-on-Trent
Frisby
Coalville
Sileby
Bardon Hill
Syston junctions
Oakham
To Peterborough
Stamford
Leicester
Manton Junction
Ketton
Knighton South Jct.
Wigston junctions
To Nuneaton
Kibworth
Corby
Market Harborough
Glendon South Junction
Desborough
Kettering
To Northampton
Wellingborough   To London

NORTH

0   10   20 miles

The map generally represents the situation in the 1970s onwards with the emphasis on locations illustrated or mentioned in the text. Some stations and other detail have been omitted to maintain clarity.

INTRODUCTION

In the mid 1970s with full-time studies completed, leading to employment and the funds to acquire a car, the opportunity was suddenly available for me to pursue railway photography in earnest. However, I saw it as more for the 'thrill of the chase' and eventually seeing the results rather than thinking the images would ever have any nostalgic value. For, by then so much had already disappeared - steam, almost a decade earlier and some of the unsuccessful diesel classes had also gone to the scrap yard. Locally, the Great Central Railway's London extension was long-closed, together with the Midland Railway's Nottingham to Melton Mowbray route and much of the Great Northern Railway's system. On some of the surviving lines, the introduction of power boxes at Derby and Trent had caused the elimination of many signal boxes and the semaphore signals they had worked.

Nevertheless, over the next few years, much leisure time was devoted to the hobby. In the course of this, I established contacts with a number of signalmen, one through a family connection, and opportunities opened up. Access to railway documentation such as Special Traffic Notices was an added bonus.

Not all main lines had given way to power signalling. Notably, the section of Midland Main Line between Loughborough and Sharnbrook was still worked in the traditional block-signalling manner, though inevitably some rationalisation of track and signals had occurred. This, the so-called 'Leicester Gap', finally came under the single control of a power box, at Leicester in 1987.

During the next 20 or so years, the East Midlands witnessed further line closures and the demise of many colliery branches. This was, from a railway system point of view, balanced to some extent by the re-opening of the Nottingham to Mansfield 'Robin Hood' direct line. This, only a few years earlier, had seemed a most unlikely possibility.

In the 1980s, many of the successful first generation diesel classes started to disappear and even the diesel multiple units gave way to shiny new replacements in the form of 'Sprinters'. This was the start of a revolution that has seen the elimination of loco-hauled passenger trains on normal services in the area.

Things continue to move on. Leicester and Trent power signal boxes have succumbed to the new East Midlands Control Centre at Derby. Its area continues to spread into hitherto mechanical signalling territory, eventually to cover 350 route miles, including nearly all the locations shown in this book. Coal trains from local collieries, once such a common sight, are now but a memory, following the closure of the region's last deep coal mine, Thoresby in Nottinghamshire, in July 2015.

The photographs contained herein are a personal view of the East Midlands. The vast majority of these were taken in the 1970s and 1980s, as the title states. However, a few images from the two following decades, mainly ones taking advantage of opportunities not available in the 1970s and 1980s, are also included.

Sadly, not all lines were visited and in some instances for those that were, poor lighting conditions or badly deteriorating film prevent their inclusion. The reader will detect a bias towards the Nottingham area. It being my home city, I could capture local scenes on short trips, often taking advantage of optimum sunlight. As with other photographers, even the constraints of a working day did not prevent photos being taken; on summer evenings and more occasionally, mornings and the odd lunchtime.

I hope that this selection of photographs will entertain. What were everyday scenes pre-dominate, but a sprinkling of 'specials' adding the unusual to the mix has also been included.

Graham Jelly Nottingham November 2017

Tuesday 21st March 1977. Trent: This is an appropriate place to commence our journey, as Trent can be considered the hub of the East Midlands. It became a junction in 1840 when the Midland Counties Railway chose to strike south from its one year-old Derby to Nottingham line, to Rugby via Leicester to connect with the London and Birmingham Railway. A 13 miles-long line going north through the Erewash Valley to Codnor Park was opened in 1847, followed by an interchange station serving north-south and east-west lines, opening on 1st May 1862. After the station's closure on 1st January 1968, Trent power signal box (PSB), seen from a passing train, continued the name. On commissioning in September 1969, it took control of 74 route miles, but in turn, was replaced by the East Midlands Control Centre in Derby, closure being on 19th July 2013.

Sunday 3rd July 1983. Trent: Class 45s 45108 and 45150 are super power for the 1305 Nottingham to St Pancras - a regular double-header. The train is passing under the bridge carrying the Trent and Toton Goods Line, which extends to Toton Yard, just over a mile to the north. The commissioning in 1901 of the 'high level goods line'- the later, more familiar name, which kept freights to and from goods lines to the south clear of the maze of lines, was the culmination of 61 years of development of the layout here. Seconds afterwards the train would pass the site of Trent station, but all traces of the single island platform had been swept away in the track rationalisation and re-alignment scheme of 1968.

(*previous page*) **Friday 21st October 1983**. **Trowell Junction**: On the Derbyshire/Nottinghamshire border, 31144 and 31173 heading along the Erewash Valley line on the Up goods, are approaching the junction with a mixed freight, no doubt bound for Toton. These yard-to-yard freights generally contained a varied selection of wagons: this one includes some PCA 51-ton straight-tanked cement hoppers. Previously, the view here would have been very different, with a second Down goods line plus a siding both on the left and a coal tip in the distance, all now returning to nature. The Erewash Valley is the western extremity of the coalfield. The seams, which tilt upwards from the east, were only just below the surface, thus mines were numerous.

Saturday 11th February 1978. Trent: One of the features of the 1969 resignalling scheme which led to Derby and Trent PSBs taking control of much of the immediate area, was that many signal boxes were initially retained as 'shunting frames'; working by release from the power box, to provide local control for sidings or, as here, a level crossing. The former Long Eaton Junction, dating from 1893, is being passed by 45122 with the 1312 ex St Pancras. By now, BR had lifted the chord to North Erewash Junction on the Erewash Valley line as a similar link from Attenborough Junction to Meadow Lane Junction on the 'high level goods line' had duplicated it. The box lasted only another five months, Trent thereafter controlled the crossing utilising then emerging technology in the form of CCTV.

Saturday 7th May 1977. Attenborough: Another box and gates survived at Attenborough station, two miles east of Trent. A Class 102 Metro-Cammell three-car DMU set, leading a further two-car unit, passes with an eastbound special, believed to be to Spalding for the annual flower parade. This box survived until the early1980s. Level crossing safety standards have thankfully improved since 1977!

Wednesday 5th September 1984. Beeston: Class 20s 20187 and 20177 approach from the west with a permanent way train comprising Salmon bogie rail wagons. The London Midland Region 'running-in' sign survived as an additional pleasing feature of the station.

Sunday 24th June 1984. Beeston: With the Beeston Boiler Company's erstwhile factory dominating the scene, 20199 and 20198 with the 0902 Derby to Skegness have reversed onto the Up line, not quite as far back as Beeston station, in order to continue 'wrong line' under Humber Road bridge towards Nottingham. This was once a regular feature of Sunday rail travel, prior to the tendency to run replacement buses whenever engineering works cause an operational problem. In the distance are the Blue Circle cement depot and a smattering of associated PCA wagons for carrying dry cement powder.

Saturday 4th June 1983. **Beeston**: 20134 and 20173 are arriving with the 0838 Leicester to Skegness. A wide-angle lens enables a better appreciation of the Midland Railway element of the station. The station building, the original canopy and its southwest side extension are Grade II listed. The MR transferred the latter, dating from 1848, from Southwell near Newark, in 1871.

Tuesday 21st June 1983. **Beeston**: Humber Road bridge provided a good vantage point for activities at the Nottingham Freightliner Terminal. It had opened on 30th June 1969 following Dr Beeching's 1963 report *The Reshaping of British Railways*, which advocated the development of freight traffic in bulk between single termini. However, it closed on 6th April 1987. In happier times 45004 ROYAL IRISH FUSILIER leaves with the 1927 to Coatbridge Freightliner Terminal, near Glasgow.

Tuesday 8th August 2000. Beeston: Part of the largely derelict site of the freightliner terminal provides the backdrop as an immaculate Class 60 60081 ISAMBARD KINGDOM BRUNEL leaves a siding, after a short recess, with a train of processed scrap metal from the nearby Sims' yard. The locomotive had been especially repainted at Toton in mock GWR lined livery and renamed from BLEAKLOW HILL, for two EWS-sponsored open days that were held the previous weekend at Old Oak Common in London.

Wednesday 1st May 1985. Wollaton: We take a brief look at the line between Radford Junction and Trowell Junction, linking Nottingham to Sheffield and the north. Having just topped the summit of the line, the 0910 St Pancras to Sheffield HST is captured in the short stretch of open countryside on the western fringes of Nottingham. At this time, the line was under threat of complete closure, with trains due to be diverted via Beeston and the freight chord from Attenborough Junction to the 'high level goods line' south of Toton. It was actually taken out of use for a while following some track damage at Trowell, but a re-think thankfully led to its full restoration to the network.

Sunday 7th May 1978. **Radford**: 45122 leaves behind an industrial and residential landscape, now much changed, with the 1656 departure from Nottingham to Sheffield. The train is on the sharp curve round to the west after passing Radford Junction, towards Trowell. Anglo-Scottish expresses once travelled this way in conjunction with the line from Melton Mowbray to Nottingham, but that line lost virtually all its passenger trains in April 1966.

Saturday 4th March 1978. **Lenton North Junction**: This is a mile south of Radford Junction. Class 47 47343 is heading north here off the curve from Lenton South Junction with a rake of empty PCA 52-ton cement hoppers from Beeston to Earles Sidings in the Hope Valley, via the junctions at Radford and Trowell. The chord survives, albeit as a seldom-used single track. The now demolished Royal Ordnance Factory forms a rather bleak backdrop.

Monday 9th May 1983. Lenton South Junction: 45107 is getting into its stride, 1¼ miles from the station with the 1830 from Sheffield to St Pancras. A fresh locomotive had come onto this train upon reversal in Nottingham, as was normal practice, to save time running round. Prior to the closure of the Melton route, generally only secondary services to London from Nottingham had travelled via Leicester. This viewpoint, from Lenton Lane overbridge, is now lost, as the Toton Lane line of Nottingham's tram system crosses the railway just east of the road bridge.

Friday 25th April 1986. Dunkirk: Following the end of widespread use of locomotives on Midland Main Line services in May 1983, two Monday-Friday locomotive-hauled trains each way did however survive. Both went from Derby in the morning and at first, both returned to Nottingham in the early evening. An added bonus was that the trains immediately returned to Derby as empty coaching stock. Viewed from the ring road overbridge, 45119 hauls the stock from the 1635 ex St Pancras. This stretch of line has notoriety, being the scene of a fatal accident on 16th December 1971. There was a head-on collision on the Down fast line, between a coal train coming off the branch at Lenton South Junction under clear signals and a parcels train from Liverpool. Regrettably, three railwaymen lost their lives.

Saturday 18th February 1984. Lenton South Junction: Class 40 40033 is captured coming off the freight-only curve from Lenton North Junction with *THE DORE MAT* railtour. This originated at Birmingham (New Street) and had already visited Crewe, Manchester, Sheffield and Doncaster by the time it passed here. Derby, Matlock and a run through the Hope Valley were yet to come. The passengers seem to be enjoying their winter day out, but are missing a glimpse of Nottingham Castle!

Sunday 28th July 1985. **Nottingham**: After the closure of the Midland Railway's Nottingham goods yard sidings, several years elapsed before BR removed the tracks and sold the site, leaving just a four-track corridor. With nature already taking over, the 1855 Nottingham to St Pancras HST is in full acceleration mode at Mansfield Junction. On the positive side, a new road built across the railway here, provides a good view in each direction as illustrated in the following two photos.

Saturday 29th August 1992. **Nottingham**: A Class 115 Tyseley-based Derby Suburban four-car set leads a three-car unit at Mansfield Junction off the curve from Lenton North Junction, working the 0957 Sheffield to Skegness. Class 58 58016, slowly approaching on the Down goods is facing a signal check before its journey to Cotgrave Colliery with MGR empties can continue. Delays here became common in the ensuing years as the number of passenger trains using the curve increased. The 2013 resignalling addressed this problem by allowing independent operation of the two routes at the junction, allied to bi-directional working on all lines towards the station.

Saturday 29th August 1992. **Nottingham**: 58016 continues its journey after being overtaken by a three-car Class 101 DMU working the 0920 Crewe to Nottingham. As a prelude to what became almost normal in recent times, both are facing red signals at Wilford Road, indicating that routes towards the station are not yet available. Meanwhile, 58033 with its MGR empties from Staythorpe waits on the Up slow for a path through the junction towards Lenton North Junction and the Trowell line.

Sunday 5th June 1983. **Nottingham**: 20134 and 20173 approach Wilford Road overbridge with the 0825 Leicester to Skegness. To the left was the site of Nottingham shed (16A), which shut in 1966. Nottingham Goods Yard, on the right, had closed far more recently. In the distance, near Mansfield Junction, are some of the Class 317 EMU sets that were stored around Nottingham pending the resolution of an industrial dispute that was blocking their introduction on the Thameslink service, south of Bedford. In the distance, Nottingham University and the Queen's Medical Centre complete the scene.

Saturday 11th September 1982. **Nottingham**: Viewed from a convenient multi-storey car park, 20071 and 20047 restart the 1235 Skegness to Leicester for the final leg of the journey. The station building, dating from 1904, was fully restored during 2012/13 with new facilities to create a transport hub to link in with the city's extended tram system. The first Nottingham station, a terminus, was to the left of the locomotives. Up and Down goods lines, which ran to the south of the station once occupied the foreground.

Monday 25th October 1976. **Nottingham**: A typical daily scene, which ensued for twenty years from the early 1960s as a Peak waits departure time on Platform 5 with a London train. On this occasion, it is 45130 and the 1250 to St Pancras and it is attracting the attention of two youthful observers. The bridge, which had carried the Great Central Railway's London extension, was demolished in the following decade but a new bridge, once again carrying rails, has been erected in the same position, to convey tram passengers. The Nottingham Station tram stop is located on the bridge. It was brought into use on 28th July 2015, a month ahead of the full extension of the tram system.

Saturday 21st April 1984. Nottingham: 45141 stands in Platform 5 with no less a train than the recently restored *Venice Simplon Orient Express*! This was an excursion from London (Victoria). During the afternoon, the stock was stabled in the long-closed London Road (Low Level) station to allow public inspection and the purchase of souvenirs. Nottingham station lost its 'Midland' suffix after the closure of Nottingham (Victoria) in September 1967.

Sunday 25th May 1980. Nottingham: The station clock shows 0920, as 20171 and 20177 depart from Platform 1 with a Bank Holiday weekend excursion. Class 25s 25248 and 25274 in Platform 5 wait their opportunity to follow. Little doubt that both were bound for Skegness. Another locomotive-hauled train waits to head west from Platform 4. As part of the resignalling and tracks alteration programme of 2013, this end of Platform 4 has been built out to meet the through line to provide another platform face with the remainder, now Platform 5, thus becoming a very useful west-facing bay. Another alteration enabled Platform 6 (now 7) on the far left to be able to handle eastbound departures.

Monday 9th September 1991. **Nottingham**: 60081 BACK TOR with an Immingham-bound empty oil train is about to pass under London Road bridge. Beyond the bridge is 70000 BRITANNIA, which was running round its support coach while on a positioning move from Crewe to Cambridge. Having already reversed direction at Derby, there was a second reversal here to minimise tender-first running.

Saturday 4th October 1980. **Nottingham**: Stratford's 47279 crosses the Nottingham Canal prior to passing under London Road with the Harwich to Manchester (Piccadilly) 'boat train'. The Great Northern Railway's 'Low Level' and 'High Level' stations at London Road form the background, as does a factory belonging to Boots. The original station had closed to passengers in 1944, but eventually became a parcels concentration depot. The later 'High Level' station, built on the link to the Great Central Railway and Nottingham (Victoria), jointly owned by the GNR, closed in July 1967. Its building saw various commercial uses before demolition in 2006.

(*above*) **Monday 20th June 1983**. **Nottingham**: The sunlight has just about disappeared on one of the longest days of the year as 31182 arrives with the 2003 Travelling Post Office mail train from Lincoln (St Marks) to Derby, passing the former London Road Junction. BR installed the connection to the former GNR network on the left in 1969. It replaced the original, further east, which required two reversals. The GNR's Goods Yard box still controlled the yard, open for the parcels trains, and even had a two-arm somersault signal. On the far right is the Up goods line, on the site of the lifted line to Melton Mowbray. The occupants of the yard: of classes 20, 25, 45 and 47, together with a Class 120 DMU are exactly as one would expect for that era.

(*above*) **Thursday 14th February 1985. Nottingham:** A telephoto lens has been used to capture 58017 with a MGR to Staythorpe. East Midland Trains' maintenance depot now occupies the area on the left. The original link to the GNR system was via a line from what is here the Down goods loop; the former exchange sidings are to the right of the locomotive. The parcels depot and yard closed in April 1986, after which the National Railway Museum claimed the somersault signal. After a rather chequered post-railway history, the Grade II listed London Road (Low Level) station is now a health club.

(*previous page lower*) **Saturday 2nd February 1980. Nottingham:** The same footbridge was used to see 40078 with a Blackpool to Thetford troop special passing the former Midland Railway's Sneinton Junction signal box, by then a 'shunting frame' supervising three level crossings. BR removed the Up goods loop, diverging to the left, soon afterwards, but the box lasted as such until 20th July 2013. Network Rail now deploys it as a training facility at Tuxford, in the north of the county. 40078 had worked light engine from Peterborough to Nottingham to take over this train. Both these images are the reverse view of the top photograph on page 19.

Saturday 16th August 1980. **Nottingham**: In the suburb of Sneinton, 25127 and 25137 with the 0835 Derby to Yarmouth have just passed under the bridge that once carried the GNR's Grantham to Nottingham line. BR retained a single line on the bridge as a headshunt to enable the parcels trains to reverse before and after visiting the depot at London Road and one such train is visible. Utilising running powers over the GNR, the LNWR then had a short branch from here to its goods station. The waste incinerator at Eastcroft, built on the track bed of the former MR Melton Mowbray line, dominates the background.

Saturday 5th March 1977. **Carlton**: A busy scene, as a Class 120 Swindon Cross Country DMU calls with the 1020 Crewe to Lincoln (St Marks). Barriers replaced the gates in 1977 and in 1980 nearby Netherfield Junction, which we will see later in the journey, took control of the crossing using CCTV. The starter signal was kept at danger for stopping trains until they were ready for departure, in conjunction with the working of the automatic half barriers at Stoke Lane crossing.

Monday 7th April 1980. Carlton: The DMU-dominated Nottingham to Lincoln line usually saw just a few locomotive-hauled excursions per year. 47050, with an Easter Monday special from Kidderminster to Cleethorpes, is having to wait for the block section to Lowdham, 4½ miles away, to clear. Formerly 'Carlton and Netherfield', the latter was dropped by BR to avoid confusion with nearby Netherfield station on the former GNR Grantham line. Netherfield sprung up following the arrival of the GNR and its Colwick Depot and marshalling yard. However, the MR got here first, in 1846, with the opening of its Nottingham to Lincoln line.

Friday 20th May 1977. Burton Joyce: A Class 114 Derby Works DMU, with an appropriate destination, arrives with the 1827 from Lincoln (St Marks). The River Trent is just visible on the right and the 1910-built box, two miles east of Carlton, like Attenborough seen earlier, unusually had a brick base, similarly to minimise the effects of flooding. It had become a gate box (i.e. no longer a block post) in October 1970. BR abolished it in 1984. The crossing became an 'open' one but now has automatic half barriers.

(*right*) **Sunday 1st June 1980. Lowdham**: Class 120 DMUs dominated the line for many years. Here, viewed from the 1930s Lowdham bypass, the 1734 Lincoln (St Marks) to Crewe is departing. In May 1988 barriers replaced gates on the level crossing with the old road through the village. A colour light, prior to the bridge, later replaced the tall signal that had co-acting arms to aid visibility. The end of the box and remaining semaphores came on 1st October 2016 when the territory of the East Midlands Control Centre at Derby was extended.

Friday 18th March 1977. Thurgarton: Almost perfect lighting illuminates Thurgarton's Down MR distant as 45005 passes with 100-ton oil tanks from Immingham to the West Midlands. This remains a staple traffic flow on this line. By this time, Thurgarton, two miles east of Lowdham, had 'gate crossing' status. Gates and signals disappeared in March 1982 when, like Burton Joyce, it became an open crossing and later, when these fell out of favour, automatic half barriers.

Monday 26th June 1978. Staythorpe: 31215 passes with the Lincoln (St Marks) to Derby mail. This and the overnight return were the only booked Class 1 trains on the line. The friendly signalman had obligingly delayed returning the home signal to danger. This once quiet spot had become busy when the first power station at Staythorpe opened in 1950. Though also erected in 1950, thus by BR, the signal box was of LMSR design having apparently come from storage at Crewe.

Friday 30th June 1978. Staythorpe: Though taken rather unwisely through the glass, the view east nevertheless gives quite a reasonable impression of the layout, as another Class 120 DMU is seen, with the 1929 Lincoln (St Marks) to Derby. A second power station (B) opened in 1962 on the north side of the line, necessitating a small extension to the box. The power stations closed in 1983 and 1994 respectively. A gas-fired power station now occupies the site. The box closed on 5th November 2016.

Thursday 23rd June 1977. Newark (Castle): In evening sunlight, 47106 passes with empty oil tanks for Immingham. The signal box dated from 1912. A second, larger signal box was once necessary to assist with controlling the extensive sidings as befitting an important market town, but a derailed locomotive demolished it in 1964. After this, the station box, three-quarters of a mile to the west of Newark Crossing, had sole control of the ever-dwindling layout. There was once a jointly owned connection to the GNR line, suitable only for transfer freights, as the connection was off a siding. As with Staythorpe Crossing, the signal box closed on 5th November 2016, forming the limit of control by the East Midlands Control Centre. It is situated within the Newark Conservation Area. (*below*) A last look at the Lincoln mail, in the charge of 31168, the arrival of which is clearly awaited. By then this was the train's only call between Lincoln and Nottingham. The working had originally been to Tamworth, to connect with the Up and Down *West Coast Postal* trains, but rationalisation later took it to Derby and a connection with the Peterborough-Crewe TPO. The return working was in the early hours. The service, which dated from the 1840s, ended in 1991.

Thursday 30th July 1981. **Newark Crossing**: 31320 and 31328 are just about to block the view of Newark's St. Mary Magdalene church spire as they noisily cross the Newark Dyke of the River Trent, working hard with the same service seen at Newark (Castle) - empty oil tanks from Kingsbury to Humber Oil Refinery. The rake comprises 51-ton wagons of TOPS code TUA. BR tabled the Nottingham to Lincoln passenger service for closure under initial Beeching proposals, but the plan was quickly reversed. Paths for Lincoln-line trains across the East Coast Main Line are at a premium and a flyover for east-west traffic has been under consideration for many years.

Sunday 1st February 1981. **Newark Crossing**: The trailing power car of the 1300 London (Kings Cross) to Edinburgh (Waverley) HST is seen just clearing the former MR. Its line to Lincoln preceded the GNR's line by six years. The latter was responsible for building the signal box, which the MR staffed and maintained. A replacement GNR box, seen here, dated from 1870 and was at this time the oldest surviving box on BR. To reflect the origins, it retained the name 'GN Crossing' until 1965, at which time BR added an east to south curve to the layout. Control passed to Doncaster PSB in May 1981.

Wednesday 18th August 1999. **Newark Crossing**: In the late 1990s, Class 55 Deltics re-appeared on the network, and not just working enthusiasts' specials. Viewed from the Newark bypass bridge, built after the BR Deltic era, D9009 ALYCIDON has just crossed over the River Trent and the Nottingham to Lincoln line with a return Ebor race meeting special from York to London (Victoria) using the VSOE rake.

Tuesday 26th August 1980. **Newark (North Gate)**: 16 months before the final withdrawal of Deltics in regular service, 55005 PRINCE OF WALES' OWN REGIMENT OF YORKSHIRE makes a typically impressive departure with the 0805 Kings Cross to Hull. By this time, BR had altered the tracks to the north of the station to allow trains to and from the Lincoln line to be independent of the main lines. Newark's position on the superbly engineered ECML ensures it enjoys much quicker journey times to and from London than are achievable from other places in the East Midlands like Derby and Nottingham, due to the winding nature of the Midland Railways' line, which we will see later.

Friday 3rd December 1976. Newark (North Gate): BR eliminated the semaphores here during the following year, but for now Class 37 37137 with a Colwick to Lindsey Oil Refinery, Immingham, empty oil tanker train has Newark South's branch home at clear. This permitted a run through the station on the Down main. At Newark Crossing, it will use the 1965-built curve onto the Midland Railway's line to Lincoln. The branch, from Bottesford, had lost its passenger service in September 1939, but a bay platform for such trains retained its track at this time.

(*opposite bottom*) **Tuesday 26th August 1980.** **Newark**: 47041 passes under Clay Lane, near to Newark South with another Colwick-Lindsey empty oil tank train. The line to here from Bottesford West Junction on the Nottingham to Grantham line was the last surviving and northernmost part of a railway system that ran as far south as the LNWR's Market Harborough to Peterborough line. The GNR and LNWR jointly owned most of it, but the section north of Bottesford was solely GNR. The latter also had exclusive ownership of a branch off it to Leicester, where it provided a rather lavish six-platform terminus, which became known as Leicester (Belgrave Road).

(*right*) **Friday 25th May 1979. Newark**: 47215 approaches Lowfield, two miles south of Newark with more Lindsey-bound tanks. There were once a total of four sidings and short works branches on either side of the line; the course of one can just be discerned above the lower signal arm. The branch was perhaps a rather surprising survivor, but after the opening of the curve at Newark in 1965, it formed part of a very convenient new route for the oil trains, obviating the need for a mid-journey reversal. A rail-served gypsum works a few miles further south, at Kilvington also generated some revenue.

Friday 7th September 1979. Newark: Lowfield signalman Jim Lane is just about to pass the single line token to the driver of 08183, working a rake of 21-ton wagons behind the leading special item, on the Kilvington trip from Newark. On first meeting him, he advised that this was the wrong place to see trains! At this time, there were three oil trains each way per day between Colwick and Immingham, plus the Kilvington trip; but three of these were timed quite close together. After closure of Newark South box in February 1980, Lowfield fringed Doncaster PSB and thus had some rather incongruous state of the art equipment installed.

(*right*) **Friday 23rd June 1978. Bottesford North Junction**: Now in Leicestershire, seven miles south of Lowfield, 31284 is nearing the half-mile curve to Bottesford West Junction with Colwick-bound oil tankers. BR singled the line to here from Lowfield in 1962. During the early 1980s, it was opened at night for trains diverted from the former MR route between Netherfield Junction and Newark, which could thus be closed for one shift to cut costs; relatively high, due to its many level crossings. However, this was short lived and the branch closed on 26th April 1987. The oil trains still run, but now require one or two reversals depending on which longer route, via Grantham or Nottingham, they take.

(*below*) **Thursday 12th July 1979. Bottesford West Junction**: 25264 and 25267 pass the box and junction signal with the return 1850 Skegness to Leicester, This and a Derby train ran Mondays to Thursdays during the school summer holidays, providing the opportunity of a day at the popular resort. The west to south curve here onto the GN and LNW Joint main line was soon found to be superfluous due to an alternative route, from Saxondale Junction to Stathern Junction, being available. However, after the closure of that in 1962, the curve, which, had been primarily used throughout its existence as a refuge siding, was fully reinstated until final closure in 1970.

Friday 28th September 1979. Bottesford West Junction: Looking east from Orston Lane crossing, 31284, is signalled onto the Newark branch with the empty oil tanker train seen on the front cover. This angle offers a good view of a steel carrier acting as a barrier between the loco and the tanks. Prior to 1962, there was also a south to east curve at Bottesford, perhaps best known for enabling trains from Leicester (Belgrave Road) to reach the Lincolnshire resorts of Skegness and Mablethorpe. After the abolition of the box on 28th November 2015, the East Midlands Control Centre now fringes with Allington, five miles to the east.

Saturday 2nd July 1977. Belvoir: This was where a branch formerly serving several ironstone quarries joined the Nottingham to Grantham line. The once considerable traffic from here declined in the 1960s but there was a brief revival in the late 1970s. 37111 hurries past with the 0720 Sheffield to Skegness. The signal box closed at the beginning of 1979, just a few years short of its centenary. The colour light Down distant, which is just visible, was for Bottesford West Junction. Unusually, it was sited below Belvoir's semaphore starter.

(*left*) **Friday 16th May 1980. Gonerby Tunnel**: We stray briefly into Lincolnshire for a glimpse of the 560 yards-long Gonerby Tunnel, two miles west of Grantham. The A1 overbridge provided the vantage point for the sight of 25212 with the lunchtime Peterborough to Crewe parcels train accelerating to the 60 mph line speed, helped by the falling 1 in 178 gradient towards Allington Junction.

(*below*) **Saturday 29th July 1978. Bingham**: The foot crossing here would be blocked for a few minutes as 37095, approaching with the 0747 Sheffield to Skegness, was to be held at the starter signal, as usual for the duration of this timetable, waiting for a DMU to clear the block section to Bottesford West Junction. At this time no Skegness loco-hauled trains made a station call here, but such a train might have been quite popular as it is an inconvenient nine miles from Nottingham. The line on the left was a short refuge siding. BR later replaced the impressive tall lattice post Down home signal with another semaphore on a shorter post.

Saturday 5th May 1979. **Bingham**: No passengers for his one either as Stratford's silver-roofed 47019 passes a youthful admirer, at line speed under the original GNR footbridge, with the 0728 Harwich (Parkeston Quay) to Manchester (Piccadilly) 'boat train'. The Ambergate, Nottingham, Boston, and East Junction Railway had constructed the line between Grantham and Nottingham in 1850 but it was leased to the GNR in 1861. Bingham once had a second station, on the GN and LNWR Joint system, but trains between Nottingham (Victoria) and Northampton (Castle) ceased to call there in July 1951, two years before the line's passenger service was withdrawn.

Saturday 5th September 1981. **Bingham**: 45124, viewed from the station footbridge, approaches, having descended at 1 in 176 from Saxondale, with the 0851 Leicester to Skegness. Bingham once warranted two signal boxes but the other one, nearer the station, closed as early as 1922. As with Bottesford West Junction, the box, which also controlled a busy level crossing, closed on 28th November 2015, having fringed with the East Midlands Control Centre at Derby since 2013.

Saturday 20th October 1979. **Saxondale**: A refurbished Class 114 DMU passes with the 1034 Nottingham to Skegness. The formation of the Grantham to Nottingham line from Radcliffe-on-Trent to Saxondale Junction, a mile west of Bingham, where the west to south link to the main GN and LNWR Joint line diverged, was four-track. After BR reduced it to two in 1962, the Derby Technical Centre used the vacated area as a test bed for various designs of paved track, reputedly in preparation for the Channel Tunnel. The Down track was slewed onto the experimental track accordingly.

Thursday 24th June 1976. Rectory Junction: The signal box here enjoyed a lofty position. Courtesy of a friendly signalman, 47019 is seen again from the box, with the return boat train the 1515 Manchester (Piccadilly) to Harwich (Parkeston Quay). The rake included a Gresley buffet car at that time. Though it had closed in 1970, Colwick Yard still from this angle presented a busy appearance as some sidings were used for the storage of weekend coaching stock and the former main line into the yard and on to the Derbyshire and Nottinghamshire coalfields was retained for a short distance as access to the Total Oil terminal. However, this merely screened the scene of desolation that lay to the west.

Friday 16th July 1976. **Rectory Junction**: Framed by the Up home signal, 47327 approaches from Cotgrave with a loaded MGR. The left hand arm was for the right hand-running 'avoiding line' that ran from Colwick East Junction but was now a truncated emergency-use siding. The signal carries a plate indicating a telephone was not provided, but that some other means, in this case a fireman's plunger, was available, so that the signaller could be alerted of the presence of a waiting train under Rule 55 - a crucial safety precaution. BR carried out some remodelling of the layout here during the following month. Further changes were only of a subtle nature, until the box closed on 28th July 2013, after 125 years of service.

Tuesday 13th August 1991. **Colwick**: A celebrity locomotive at the Colwick Total Oil terminal: 47401, the pioneer Brush Type 4, D1500, which entered service in September 1962. Two months earlier, its home depot, Immingham had given it a close approximation of the original livery and the fitting name STAR OF THE EAST. Such a livery variation would have been unthinkable in the 1970s. Withdrawal came in June 1992. It is preserved at the Midland Railway-Butterley, being now named NORTH EASTERN, which it carried in the 1980s. Here it awaits a return to base with oil empties.

Monday 23 August 1976. **Rectory Junction**: As mentioned in the Belvoir caption, there was a brief revival of iron ore traffic from there in the late 1970s. To add to the retro effect, the locomotives of this working, 20156 and 20164, are still in green livery. The rake comprises 33½-ton HKV ironstone hoppers. The locomotives are about to pass the signal box, out of shot to the left. Some people will remember the long hot summer of 1976 when special measures were required to feed livestock.

Saturday 13th August 1983. Rectory Junction: The same location, as 37093 cautiously brings the 1105 Skegness to Sheffield over the original 1850 Trent bridge - by this time having been strengthened and refurbished - and its red brick arches, now a Grade II listed structure. East of this was originally a timber viaduct, which was an early 20th century conversion to engineering brick, while the 1960s link to Cotgrave Colliery was carried over the flood plain on a concrete structure. The colliery ceased production in 1993, after 29 years. A south to east curve from the Cotgrave branch had an even shorter life than that; BR took it out of use in the mid 1970s, it having seen little traffic.

Wednesday 14th July 1976. Netherfield: A typical scene as 20044 and 20176 cross Netherfield Lane, a quarter of a mile from Netherfield Station, with 16-ton (MCO) coal empties to Gedling. BR singled the line after closure of the GNR's adjoining depot, Colwick, best remembered as 38A, and marshalling yard. A shunter was employed at the crossing box here to operate the crossing and then accompany the train to and from the colliery.

Friday 10th December 1976. Netherfield: 25217 and 25212 are surprise motive power for another, rather late running, train of coal empties for Gedling Colliery. On show are two types of 21-ton wagons. To the front are standard hoppers originating from a LNER design. Behind these are some end-door opens with GWR ancestry. Seen crossing the MR Nottingham to Lincoln line, they are on the stub of the former Derbyshire Extension known locally as the 'back line'. After many years of disuse following the closure of the colliery, the rails on that were finally lifted in 2012.

Friday 27th May 1977. Colwick East Junction: In 1919, a spur was taken off the Nottingham to Grantham line at Colwick East Junction to give access to a light railway serving the adjoining Colwick Industrial Estate. This had industries dealing with such diverse products as concrete, oil and sugar. Latterly, only oil products were served by rail. Here is a typical scene as 08741 propels a very mixed rake of petrochemical wagons comprising 45 and 35-ton tanks from the exchange sidings. Some appear to be for bitumen. The main line is on the right. Closure came on 1st April 1985, and now there is only a little evidence that it ever existed.

Wednesday 30th August 1978. Colwick East Junction: The exit from the estate line is seen here, controlled since 1972 from a ground frame released by Rectory Junction. The last train of the day has long gone as 37021 comes past with the 1515 Manchester (Piccadilly) to Harwich 'boat train'. Stratford Class 47s were the usual motive power for this train as far as Sheffield where the train reversed, but 37s were not uncommon. They had been staple motive power in the days up to May 1973, when the train ran via Lincoln and Spalding.

Tuesday 4th September 1979. Colwick East Junction: The 'boat train' was something of a favourite as it was just possible to see it after work. In the rather drab blue/grey era this was as colourful as it got, as Stratford's 47169 GREAT EASTERN is seen working hard between the severe speed restrictions at Netherfield and Rectory Junction. The train was the descendent of the *NORTH COUNTRY CONTINENAL* - a train having its origins in the 19th Century. BR extended it to Edinburgh and Glasgow via Manchester (Victoria) in May 1983 as *THE EUROPEAN*, in which form it lasted for a few more years. The houses on the right were part of London North Western Terrace, a reminder that the LNWR also had a Colwick shed, in the area back from right of the locomotive

Friday 9th March 1984. Netherfield: Having just passed through the station 'wrong line' the driver of 20191 and 20077 bringing coal from Gedling Colliery has just handed over the single line token to Netherfield Junction signalman Les Fletcher, prior to taking the crossover to gain the Down line. The 21-ton hoppers were still in original condition and were by this time something of an endangered species. The colliery closed in 1991. At its zenith in the 1960s, the box controlled routes going off in five directions. It was a fringe signal box to Trent PSB.

Saturday 21st August 1976. Netherfield: Traditionally, the first train to return from Skegness was that for Sheffield. 37108 passes through the station, which still retained some semaphores. The branch to the left was one arm of a triangle at the start of the Derbyshire Extension, which took the GNR to Derby and ultimately Stafford, plus branches into the Nottingham and Derbyshire coalfields - its prime purpose. It was severed in April 1960, when BR rather controversially closed the subsidence-damaged Mapperley Tunnel, just beyond Gedling Colliery.

Saturday 28th June 1986. Netherfield: The mid 1980s saw the introduction of loco hauled cross-country trains as the start of 'Regional Railways'. 31435 passes Netherfield Junction box with the 0720 Blackpool (North) to Harwich (Parkeston Quay). The semaphore was fixed, designating the end of the brief wrong line running for trains from Gedling. BR opened the non-standard signal box in 1960 and later it controlled the 1965-opened link to the Nottingham to Lincoln line, which enabled Grantham services to be run into Nottingham (Midland) in lieu of 'Victoria'. The line had connected to the MR's when built in 1850; the junction was removed in 1857, when the ANB & EJR opened its own Nottingham station at London Road. The signal box closed on 28th July 2013 and was demolished a year later.

Tuesday 23rd July 1985. **Radford Junction**: We switch across the city to the Robin Hood line. Class 56 56062 heads south from the then former Mansfield route with a MGR from one of the four remaining collieries served by the branch. The last, Calverton, closed in April 1999. The line from Trowell Junction is converging from the left. Radford Station, here, closed with the Mansfield passenger service on 12th October 1964, but was not re-opened as part of the Robin Hood line scheme.

Friday 27th April 1984. **Basford**: A long wait extending to two evenings was finally rewarded by the sight of 47356 heading north. It is about to pass under the Nottingham ring road with MGR empties. The scene is now much changed with Nottingham Express Transit's Line 1, which opened in March 2004, having two tracks between the railway and the River Leen. In the distance, the gasholder has been demolished and the headquarters and depot of the tram system now lie just beyond the rear of the train. There are no coal trains either!

Saturday 10th February 1979. **Basford**: 20030 and 20043 are passing the connection to Babbington Colliery as they approach Lincoln Street crossing with *THE NOTTINGHAMSHIRE COLLIER*, a tour that originated at London (St Pancras) but returned to Marylebone. It turns out this date was virtually half way between closure to passenger services on 12th October 1964 and re-opening of the first stage of the Robin Hood line to Newstead, on 17th May 1993. The tracks of Line 1 of the tram system now run parallel, to the left. The box, which fringed Trent PSB, closed on 29th September 2001. Railtrack transferred it the same night to Leicester, just north of the station, where it became a training facility for the Signal and Telegraph Department. In 2014, the structure was moved to the Rushden, Higham and Wellingborough Railway.

(*left*) **Monday 27th August 2001. Bulwell**: A Class 156 DMU is arriving with the 1656 Worksop to Nottingham. The station here, on the site of the original, Bulwell (Market), opened on 23rd May 1994, a year after the restoration of passenger services to the line. Until October 2001, there were Up and Down platforms, but through Bulwell there was insufficient space to locate the parallel tramline elsewhere and so the Down line was removed to as far as just south of the station. Thus, the remaining platform serves Up and Down trains. NET has an island platform, at the start of its own single line section (except for the island platform stops) going north to the two-track terminus at Hucknall.

Wednesday 26th August 1981. Bulwell: Looking south from Moor Bridge, 20134 and 20195 approach Bestwood Park Junction with empty 21-ton hoppers, mainly rebodied, along the alignment of the present day tramline. The Robin Hood line, which here has a passing loop to break the extended single line section to the south, occupies the more than adequate former sidings and nature has reclaimed the rest. The Great Central Railway's impressive viaduct, disused since 1966, forms the skyline. The end for that came just a few years later.

(*right*) **Wednesday 26th August 1981. Bulwell**: Looking north from the same bridge: 47356 brings a loaded MGR past Bestwood Park Junction signal box. The sidings here dealt with some of the trains to and from the various collieries just to the north. In 1952, BR opened a line to the new Calverton Colliery a few miles to the east. It branched off just north of here, necessitating the remodelling of some sidings and construction of a replacement signal box. In October 1970, BR severed the line, north of Annesley and transferred responsibility for the servicing of the remaining collieries to here from Kirkby Depot, which closed simultaneously. The signal box survived until 29th September 2001, when Trent PSB's area of control was extended.

Saturday 16th May 1992. Kirkby-in-Ashfield: Following severance of the line, the 199 yards-long Kirkby Tunnel was filled with spoil. The five times-longer former Great Central Railway's tunnel, the site of the approach cutting to which can be identified by the lighter grass to the left of the building, was also filled. This allowed coal mining to proceed underneath them. Key to the feasibility of the entire Robin Hood line project was the condition of the shorter tunnel and at the time of this photo, a recent trial excavation had thankfully revealed the 1848-built structure to be in excellent condition.

Saturday 15th February 1997. Kirkby-in-Ashfield: Just under five years later, Class 33s 33116 HERTFORDSHIRE RAILTOURS and 33156 SHAKESPEARE CLIFF are about to enter the tunnel with *THE ROBIN RELIANT* railtour, bound ultimately for Scarborough. Not meeting 1990s standards, the former double track tunnel was now only available for a single line. Specials have been rare, as there are pathing difficulties due to the intensive use of the single line from Bulwell to Kirkby, albeit partly relieved from 2001 by a further passing loop, at Newstead.

(*above*) **Saturday 16th May 1992. Kirkby-in-Ashfield**: The approach cutting at the north end was somewhat longer and much deeper. Though filled to ground level, fortunately, no development had taken place. However, once excavations began the engineers determined that the house to the left was too close to the cutting and it had to be acquired and demolished. The cutting had first been excavated for the opening of the line in 1848 as far as Kirkby, a year before services commenced to Mansfield.

(*left*) **Tuesday 21st May 1996. Kirkby-in-Ashfield**: A new bridge was constructed to carry the B6021 and it provides the vantage point for a view of a Class 150 Sprinter DMU at the summit of the very steep climb up the Leen Valley, emerging from under the ridge known as 'Robin Hood's Hills' with the 1500 Nottingham to Mansfield Woodhouse. This was the first spring of operation following the Stage 2 Robin Hood line re-opening in November 1995. During that year, nature, mainly in the form of gorse, wasted no time in claiming the bare soil.

(*left*) **Tuesday 21st May 1996. Kirkby- in-Ashfield**: The new line joined the existing line from Pye Bridge on the Erewash Valley line to Kirkby at what became Kirkby Lane End Junction. 58044 is seen heading a loaded MGR over the new junction towards Mansfield, no doubt heading for one of the Trent Valley power stations. The Robin Hood line is double-tracked for three-quarters of a mile prior to the tunnel, running on the site of, but at different levels to, former GNR and GCR lines.

(*below*) **Sunday 19th November 1995. Mansfield**: From 1964, Mansfield gained some notoriety as being reputedly the largest town in England without a railway station. For many years there seemed to be no solution to this, as the simple option of reaching Nottingham via existing railways, including the Erewash Valley line, would not time-wise have been competitive with the direct road alternative. To celebrate the official opening, a 'fun day' was held on the preceding Sunday. A three-car DMU comprising classes 150 and 153 has arrived with the 1158 Nottingham to Mansfield Woodhouse. The latter was chosen as the terminus for the interim Stage 2, as it had space for a turn-back platform. Happily, the former station building, seen to the left, later returned to railway use as the booking office.

(*right*) **Sunday 14th May 1995**. **Kirkby-in-Ashfield**: A station at Kirkby did not open until 18th November 1996. Here we see 37225 on an engineering train in the newly widened cutting just to the north of Kirkby Lane End Junction. This was actually on the former GNR Leen Valley Extension line, which ran north to Shirebrook and did not previously have a station in the town. BR had closed the line in 1968 and lifted the track, but using two new connections, in 1972 it became a substitute for the former MR route. This allowed the elimination of a level crossing and released town-centre land for sale.

(*below*) **Saturday 26th October 1996**. **Mansfield**: Immediately northeast of the station, an imposing viaduct carries the railway across the town. Passengers in the Class 150 DMU forming the 1158 Nottingham to Mansfield Woodhouse are near the end of their journey, but meanwhile can enjoy a rooftop autumnal view. The MR opened the extension from Mansfield to Worksop in 1875. Mansfield once had rival stations: in addition to the re-opened former 'Town' station, the 'Central' station, built by the Great Central Railway provided an alternative, albeit short-lived. Not opened until 1916, it failed to see out even a full 40 years, closing on 2nd January 1956.

Wednesday 19th August 1998. Creswell: A Class 150 DMU arrives with the 1434 Worksop to Nottingham. Formerly 'Elmton and Creswell', the re-opened station has a shorter name. The branch to Clowne and on towards Chesterfield was still signalled at this stage but had been out of use for several years. The LMSR-built signal box, dating from 1946 was subsequently permanently switched out pending formal closure. Like the other new stations on the line, the station received a striking colour scheme in accordance with the 'Robin Hood' branding.

Saturday 30th June 1984. Worksop: Trains from Nottingham once again reached Worksop, 32 miles-distant, upon the implementation of the third and final stage of the 'Robin Hood' project on 25th May 1998. They now share the station with trains on the Sheffield to Retford route. However, they were just a pipe dream when 40082 called with the much lamented, and also here clearly much enjoyed, 0815 Manchester (Piccadilly) to Skegness, some 14 years earlier.

Monday 8th October 2001. Pinxton: The line from Pye Bridge to Kirkby-in-Ashfield now sees little traffic. However, for virtually a full fortnight in 2001, Robin Hood line trains were diverted this way due to a blockade in Nottingham to allow the changes to accommodate the parallel tramline. It has subsequently taken diverted trains when incidents have caused a blockage between Kirkby and Radford Junction. A Class 156 DMU is ascending towards Kirkby with the 1114 Nottingham to Worksop. Regular passenger services ceased in 1951, though a daily Kirkby to Nottingham and return so-called workmen's train ran until September 1965.

Sunday 25th July 1982. Pinxton: Here we have a road view, looking north. The signal to the right was unusual in having a colour light distant, for Sleights Sidings East, below it. The semaphore's green spectacle was blacked out, so when it was cleared, only the colour light, which would then become illuminated, was visible. The East Midlands Control Centre incorporated this area in June 2007. The signal box now resides at the Barrow Hill Roundhouse Railway Centre near Chesterfield. The MR built a station here, Pinxton and Selston, the only one on the line. So did the GNR, at the northern end of a branch that closed in 1963.

Saturday 7th February 1981. **Toton**: The MR first laid sidings here in the 1850s to sort trains to and from the collieries and iron works reached by the Erewash Valley line, which had opened in 1847 and a locomotive depot soon followed. A new bespoke diesel depot to cater for the whole region opened early in 1965. Resident from day one was the former D4, now Class 44 44004 GREAT GABLE. To mark the imminent demise of the small class of ten original Peaks, the depot restored it to green livery and reinstated the nameplates. Later on in the year, the locomotive left for a new home at the Midland Railway-Butterley. (*below*) A *Railway Correspondence and Travel Society* visit provided the opportunity for a glimpse inside the depot of 45061 in the three-road heavy maintenance section of the overall 15 maintenance roads. When it opened, BR claimed this to be the largest depot of its type in Western Europe. It marked the end of steam practice-type shed allocations and instead the adoption of an innovative (and ultimately flawed) 'common user' policy for the growing diesel fleet on the Midland lines of the London Midland Region, a responsibility shared with Cricklewood in London.

(*above*) **Tuesday 14th June 1983**. **Toton**: The high bank to the east of the yard provides a fine vantage point. Here, looking southwest we see the Up side departure roads for the south, the wagons having been sorted using gravity, by 'hump shunting'. The yard reached its zenith in 1950 when BR opened the expanded and remodelled the Up side. The LMSR had dealt with the Down side in 1938. This lies beyond the main through lines and Toton Centre signal box. These schemes had introduced the use of mechanical retarders to control the speed of wagons, previously achieved manually by 'chasers' having to run alongside to pin down the brakes; the adverse health and safety aspects of which requiring little imagination! The landmark power station at Ratcliffe-on-Soar is on the horizon.

(*left*) **Saturday 26th May 1984**. **Toton**: A friend knew someone in high authority at the depot who gave permission for some visits. 58001, then just over a year into service, occupies the fuelling bay. The depot was provided with fuel storage facilities commensurate with the large number of locomotives in its care. Prior to the diesel depot, facilities at Toton were based around a traditional roundhouse shed. BR had quickly discovered that such facilities were unsuitable for diesels, which had differing needs; being far more susceptible to the dirt and very low winter temperatures synonymous with the steam shed environment. This led to a countrywide wave of diesel depot construction.

Saturday 26th May 1984. **Toton**: A surprise sight was the former British Thomson Houston Type 1, D8237. This dated from 1957 and designated by BR under TOPS as Class 15. It was one of four class survivors, as self-propelled carriage heating units. Numbered ADB 968002, this use endured from 1969 until 1981, at a variety of locations. The transfer to Toton was to provide parts for a sister unit DB988000 (D8243), following formal withdrawal in November 1982. It was scrapped the next year at Attercliffe, Sheffield. However, one of the four, D8233 has been preserved.

Thursday 26th September 1985. **Toton**: 47147 has charge of a Down train of empty 45-ton HEA coal hoppers heading straight through the yard on the Erewash Valley main line. The many bulk-movement freights by this time heading directly back and forth between a single supplier and a single customer, a trend encouraged in the 1963 *Reshaping of British Railways* by Dr Beeching, highlighted the increasing obsolescence of the steam-age marshalling yard. In particular, the changing pattern of coal traffic resulting from the decline in the use of domestic coal was concurrent with the increased demand for electricity. This led to the increase in the number of ever-larger coal-burning power stations, served by efficient MGR trains not needing re-sorting en-route.

(*opposite bottom*) **Thursday 26th September 1985. Toton**: 31175 heads away for the south on the Up goods towards Trent. It is passing under the bridge that carried the Down arrival lines leading from the 'high level goods line' over the main lines and into the yard. Trent East Junction signal box can be seen just left of centre. It was the same age as Toton Centre; both were further examples of boxes that BR retained as 'shunting frames' to control movements in the various yards while Trent PSB signalled the main lines.

Thursday 26th September 1985. Toton: This is the reverse view of the panoramic scene on page 51. 31175 is captured leaving for the south from the West Yard with a rake of engineer's fleet Plaice ballast wagons, dating from the late 1970s. 37211 and 37134 wait with steel from Lackenby (Teeside) to Corby. The wagon repair shop is in the background. Toton Centre signal box, built by BR in 1949 is just visible, but only the base of Toton Junction signal box, which the train is passing, remained. Just left of centre, beneath the bank, is the Up side control tower, from where the hump shunting was operated. This also incorporated, on the lower of three floors, all the electrical and mechanical equipment for the process of hump shunting. Toton is the chosen location for a station serving Derby and Nottingham on HS2, which is to run through here.

Saturday 23rd April 1983. Trowell Junction: 45057 brings a London (St Pancras) to Carlisle special, *THAMES-EDEN PULLMAN* past the junction with the line to Nottingham via Radford Junction. The Steam Locomotive Operators Association's 'Pullman' liveried rake indicates that this train would later enjoy true steam haulage, 46229 DUCHESS OF HAMILTON taking over for some of the return journey. Part of the remains of the giant Stanton Ironworks, once a major source of traffic for the line, lies in the background.

Saturday 12th April 1986. Trowell Junction: Another special is seen heading to Carlisle, this time from London (Victoria), via the Settle and Carlisle line, comprising a combination of classes 201 and 202 'narrow' Hasting line-gauge DEMU stock. It is passing under the road bridge from which the previous photo was taken. The railtour had the title *LONG THIN DRAG* - surely one of the most inventive railtour names of all time!

Sunday 31st May 1987. Trowell Junction: Celebrity green liveried pioneer EE Type 4, 40122/D200 heads past with a special, *COALVILLE SCRUTATOR*, from London (St Pancras) to the Midland Railway-Butterley. A pair of Class 33s had brought the tour as far as Coalville, for an open day at the BR depot. When 40122 was returned to traffic as D200 in 1983, the necessary work, which included a donor power unit as well as the repaint, was carried out at Toton Depot, just three miles to the south.

Saturday 13th June 1992. Trowell Junction: Class 50s 50050 FEARLESS and 50007 SIR EDWARD ELGAR come past with a special from London (Waterloo) to Worksop for another BR open day. The tour also visited, amongst other places, Chester, hence the train name, *THE COURT CHESTER*. 50007 is now resident at the Severn Valley Railway. Happily, 50050 the first of the class, is also preserved, as D400. This is the site of Trowell station, closed on 2nd January 1967.

Sunday 25th July 1982. Alfreton Tunnel: 45057 emerges from the 840 yards-long tunnel with the 1400 Sheffield to St Pancras. The parapet of the disused tunnel, which once housed the goods lines, is just visible. This is on a second extension to the Erewash Valley line, which opened on May 1st 1862 from Pye Bridge. Together, they added nine miles to the original line. The first station to be re-opened on the line, Alfreton and Mansfield Parkway, the former Alfreton and South Normanton, is just north of the tunnel.

Sunday 25th July 1982. Westhouses: 47536 passes Tibshelf Sidings with the 1621 Sheffield to Harwich (Parkeston Quay). The semaphore signals here mainly belonged to Tibshelf East Junction (out of sight to the right) on a branch serving several collieries. The exception was the distant facing north which was worked by Blackwell East, around the curve to Westhouses. These fringed to Trent PSB, which signalled the main line and controlled the connections. The curious rails, diagonal to the line to the rear and beyond the train, were the remnants of research crossings installed many years previously by Derby Technical Centre.

Sunday 13th May 1983. **Westhouses**: Looking south, we have a scene typical of the whole Erewash Valley line: a mixture of urban and rural, with colliery lines joining the main artery. A southbound Class 120 DMU is on an unidentified working. The branch off to the left once led to Westhouses MPD but by then served only New Hucknall Colliery. This is the site of Westhouses and Blackwell station another that closed with the end of the Nottingham to Sheffield local service, on 2nd January 1967. Of the other closures on this date, Langley Mill (previously Langley Mill and Eastwood) re-opened in 1986, 13 years after Alfreton and Mansfield Parkway, while another, on the site of Ilkeston (Junction) opened in April 2017.

Saturday 6th April 2002. **Clay Cross**: Deltic 9016 GORDON HIGHLANDER, running north over George Stephenson's North Midland Railway from Derby with a railtour from Crewe to Scarborough, sweeps round the curve at the junction with the Erewash Valley line. This was the limit of the 1862 extension. A new north-south route was created upon linking with the Derby to Leeds line, which had opened in 1840, Opinions on the locomotive's livery will vary but it was at least sympathetic to the lines of the locomotive, as well as being very striking.

Saturday 12th April 2003. **Clay Cross**: 60035 heads a freight comprising BBA and BAA steel carriers loaded with billets along the Up main. Clay Cross station was here. Built in 1940, the MR later expanded it to four platform faces. Unfortunately, it was almost two miles by road from the town, that being situated above the one mile-long tunnel on the Derby line. It, too, was a 2nd January 1967 casualty along with the stations on the Erewash Valley line. This location was just 2½ miles from the northern limit of Trent PSB's area of control, fringing with Sheffield PSB. (*below*) 56090 brings a Toton to Aldwarke loaded scrap train comprising SSA 35½-ton wagons along the Erewash Valley Down goods line. Unaccountably, this location was not visited until the 2000s, but nevertheless well before major remodelling of the tracks by Network Rail. Now the routes no longer merge here; instead, they operate as separate lines until just south of Chesterfield.

Friday 27th May 1977. **Chesterfield**: A small surviving section of the former Lancashire, Derbyshire and East Coast Railway's viaduct provided a vantage point for 45141 leaving the station with the 1210 Sheffield to St Pancras. The Up and Down goods lines are visible, curving behind the station. A third, bi-directional, platform served by what is now generally the Down slow line was opened in July 2010. The Great Central Railway's Chesterfield loop-line ran from bottom right before a tunnel took it to the town's 'Central' station, so missing a view of the famous crooked spire!. (*below*) An ex works 46047 heads south with an unidentified working, but almost certainly a northeast to southwest service via Derby, which this class dominated. Chesterfield once had three stations, as in addition to the Midland Railway's station seen here and the GCR loop-line station, that company acquired a second, 'Market Place', when it absorbed the Lancashire, Derbyshire and East Coast Railway in 1907. However, the MR station was the most convenient from a strategic viewpoint and appropriately is the sole survivor.

Saturday 21st January 1978. Chesterfield: 37025 makes a call on a chilly morning with the 0730 Birmingham (New Street) to Newcastle. The shadowy remains of the LD & ECR are just visible through the frosty air. The original line north of here ran well to the east of Sheffield on its way to Leeds. It was not until 1870 that the MR opened the much more challenging, from an engineering viewpoint, line to Sheffield, over which this train is about to travel. The original route, called 'the old road', has mainly been used for freight and as a diversionary passenger line ever since. (*below*) Soon afterwards 44009 SNOWDON arrived with the *FAREWELL CLASS 44* railtour from Nottingham to Crewe and back. BR promoted this as the last railtour to feature the class. After running via 'the old road', it traversed the Woodhead route on its way to Crewe. 44008 PENYGHENT took over for the return, via the West Midlands.

Saturday 12th February 1977. South Wingfield: The rare, though not unique, sight of a Class 52 Western on BR metals in the East Midlands. In suitably sombre lighting, D1023 *WESTERN FUSILIER* climbs steadily along the original North Midlands Railway on the edge of the Peak District, with the WESTERN FINALE from Exeter (St Davids) to York. This was just two weeks before the end of the class on BR. Shortly after that, D1023 made a more permanent move to York, to become part of the national collection at the National Railway Museum.

Monday 27th May 1985. Wirksworth: The town, on the end of a branch line from Duffield on the Derby-Sheffield line, lost is passenger service in 1947. This Bank Holiday weekend saw the revival of services in the form of an enterprising series of *THE WIRKSWORTH PHOENIX* railtours, so popular they were repeated until 1987. However, the branch's core traffic, limestone, dwindled, leading to closure in December 1989. It is preserved as the Ecclesbourne Valley Railway, running the full length of the 8½ miles-long branch, though there is not now a rail connection to the main line at Duffield. A Class 150 DMU prepares to work back to Derby with the 1130 departure.

Saturday 4th July 1987. Derby: The spectacle of 45124 crossing the River Derwent, just north of Derby station with 0940 Poole to Bradford is insufficient to distract the fishermen; clearly enjoying their recreation. The fact that the locomotive was built nearby in the world-famous works will also be lost on them! This location is immediately south of Derby Junction, where the Midland Counties Railway's line from Trent joined the Derby to Sheffield route. There was also a north curve, which enabled trains to avoid Derby station.

Wednesday 8th February 1984. Derby: Derby's future as a significant railway centre was secured as early as 1836 when three companies, The Midland Counties Railway, The Birmingham and Derby Junction Railway, and the North Midland Railway were authorised to construct lines to converge on the town. Sensibly, they built a joint station and in 1844, the companies merged, creating the Midland Railway, which naturally made Derby its base. BR judged the original station building not to be capable of being modernised to suit modern standards, demolishing and replacing it in the mid 1980s.

(*right*) **Tuesday 30th May 1978**. **Derby**: The city was a convenient starting point for some of the Skegness summer trains such as the 0928 departure seen here. 20193, which was coupled to 20037, has been appropriately adorned with *JOLLY FISHERMAN* headboards on this occasion. The station has five through platforms and a south facing bay. It once had an overall roof but this was bomb damaged during WW2. A major programme of works is scheduled for 2018. This will see major capacity-building changes to the layout, particularly at the southern end of the station, an extra island platform on the eastern side and resignalling.

(*below*) **Saturday 28th November 1981**. **Derby**: Towards the end of the BR Deltic era the crowds have turned out to see 55022 ROYAL SCOTS GREY on a York to London (Paddington) special. The destination was reached via Birmingham (New Street), Cheltenham Spar and Swindon. The GNR also had a station in the MR citadel of Derby, at Friargate, on its route from Nottingham to Eggington Junction and ultimately Stafford. With the exception of seasonal trains and excursions, passenger services west of Derby ceased as early as 1939 and the surviving service, to Nottingham (Victoria) ended in September 1964. Freight traffic finished in May 1968, but part of the line west of Derby survived as a research facility until July 1990.

Saturday 9th April 1983. Derby: Normal motive power and a more usual destination, as 45107 leaves a busy station behind as it sweeps round the curve at London Road Junction with the 1219 to St Pancras. A welcome feature at this time was the Midland Railway signal box, Engine Sidings No. 2, which BR retained as a 'shunting frame' until 8th February 1987, to control access to depot and works lines. Railway enthusiasts on this train will be extra alert for the next couple of minutes with sidings adjoining the research centre, always likely to have something of interest on show, whilst the sidings around Etches Park depot were a potential source of interest on the north side of the line.

Tuesday 30th May 1978. Derby: 45107 is seen again, another loco at its place of build (as D43 in August 1961), arriving from the south. BR split construction of Class 45 between Derby and Crewe. Two further pre-grouping companies: the LNWR and the North Staffordshire Railway, both utilising running powers over the MR, also had a rather audacious tangible presence in Derby, sharing a goods depot. In addition, the LNWR had an engine shed. Access to both these facilities, on the west side of the Birmingham line was gained via a junction situated three-quarters of a mile south of the station. Signals with a 'DY' prefix dominate. Derby PSB took control of the lines radiating from Derby in the summer of 1969. Transfer of control to its very close neighbour the East Midlands Control Centre is part of the 2018 programme of works.

Monday 27th May 1985. Derby: The old and new order: Sprinter 150002 departs with the 1213 special to Wirksworth while a soon-to- be-phased-out Class 120 DMU has a further nine minutes to wait before departing 'all stations' for Matlock, the network operational limit of the former line to Manchester (Central) via Bakewell and Chinley. However, Peak Rail privately operates a four miles section northwards from a separate platform at Matlock to Rowsley South. It is a bank holiday and the rain has set in.

Saturday 9th April 1983. Spondon: 45102 is two miles east of Derby station with the 1019 Derby St Pancras. The MR built the existing line, from London Road Junction to Spondon Junction, half a mile west of here, to obviate the need for stopping through trains, to and from the north, to have to reverse at Derby. The original line perished in the 1969 track rationalisation programme that immediately preceded the commissioning of Derby PSB. However, some of the route survives, serving ballast sidings at Chaddeston, access being via Derby Junction. (*below*) A Class 120 DMU approaches with the 0920 Crewe to Lincoln (St Marks). Spondon station signal box was a notable survivor, albeit as yet another 'shunting frame', supervising a level crossing and the sidings in conjunction with the, now closed, adjoining massive British Celanese complex. BR abolished it on 19th December 1988.

Saturday 14th April 1984. **Ratcliffe-on-Soar**: Moving south of Trent, we see the former Western Region's 47078 SIR DANIEL GOOCH providing welcome, if rather surprising motive power for the 1015 Nottingham to Luton parcels. The connection to the Up goods provided a southern entry/exit for the power station. The train is passing under the bridge carrying the A453 Nottingham to M1 link, north of which is now the site of the four-platform East Midlands Parkway station.

(*left*) **Friday 30th March 1984**. **Ratcliffe-on-Soar**: 58009 attracts some youthful attention as it passes around the loop having delivered more coal to add to the stockpile. This was right at the start of the 1984/85 miners' strike. The fifty Class 58 locomotives were synonymous with the East Midlands, being maintained at Toton and doing much of their work in the region. One of the class, 58041, was named RATCLIFFE POWER STATION after this establishment, which had opened in 1968.

Saturday 19th May 1979. Ratcliffe-on-Soar: The morning southbound parcels from Nottingham, the destination of which varied over the years, was often used as a testing trip for locomotives newly out shopped from Derby works after repair. Here a pristine 25119, looking as good as it did when leaving Derby new in May 1964, pilots 45136, the destination in this timetable being Wellingborough. Beyond the short Redhill tunnels in the distance, is the River Trent and immediately north of that, Trent Junction, where the routes to Derby and Nottingham diverge.

(*opposite top*) **Friday 20th April 1984. Ratcliffe-on-Soar:** 56071 creeps around the loop prior to setting off northwards with the newly emptied 32-ton capacity HAA wagons, illustrating the principle of non-stop merry-go-round working. To assist the driver while on these operations, these locomotives have a subsidiary speedometer calibrated to show 0 to 3 mph only.

(*opposite bottom*) **Friday 8th May 1987. Ratcliffe-on-Soar:** The road is set for 58038 to cross from the Down goods into the power station with the late afternoon arrival of the fly ash empties back from Fletton just south of Peterborough. Fly ash is a waste product of coal-fired electricity generation and was for a long time dumped in landfill at Fletton but these trains no longer run and this connection to the main line has been removed.

(*page 70 upper*) **Saturday 19th May 1979. Ratcliffe-on-Soar**: Spring is in the air to greet 47547, about to pass the power station with a rather short rake forming the 0813 St Pancras to Derby. The train is descending a gentle gradient of 1 in 497 whilst taking the easy curves at high speed, both being characteristic engineering features of the original Midland Counties Railway's route between Trent and Rugby. The MR quadrupled the line in the 1870s. The Up and Down goods lines to the left have, as far north as Trent South Junction been upgraded to 'slow line' designation in recent years, for regular use by passenger trains.

Friday 8th May 1987. Ratcliffe-on-Soar: Looking south again, but this time in late afternoon, 37508 and 37511 are typical power for a Corby to Lackenby train of steel empties. This train would continue on the Down goods line and onto the 'high level goods line' at Trent; keeping it clear of the passenger-carrying line. Though freight traffic has declined, so passenger trains have increased in frequency and thus the 'high level goods line' continues to perform an important role in the modern era.

Friday 10th March 1978. **East Leake**: The Great Central had long-since closed as a main line but there was, and still is, some freight activity via the 1974-built chord linking it with the Midland Railway's line at Loughborough. 45065 evokes memories as it sweeps around the island platform, returning the second trip working of the day to Leicester from the Ministry of Defence complex at Ruddington and the gypsum works at Hotchley Hill, adjacent to Rushcliffe Halt, a mile or so north of here. In the consist are a number of vans, open wagons and some Warwell wagons of 50-ton capacity, built to carry Sherman tanks in WW2. To the right is what remained of the goods yard. The station had closed to passengers on 5th May 1969, with the end of the twilight Nottingham (Arkwright Street) to Rugby (Central) service.

Friday 20th July 1979. **Ruddington**: Following the closure of the MOD depot in 1985, the site has been developed as the Nottingham Transport Heritage Centre, the base of the northern section of the preserved Great Central: now a fully-fledged preserved railway. South of Rushcliffe Halt the privately owned line is also still effectively part of the national network, serving the gypsum works. 25127 is seen upon arrival, prior to reversing the train of 21-ton wagons into the ordnance complex. This manoeuvre is perpetuated today in preservation.

Friday 10th March 1978. Kegworth: The ten Derby-built pioneer Peaks, later Class 44s, were based at Toton from the early 1960s. A typical duty was the Toton to Whitemoor service. 44005, formerly CROSS FELL passes the site of Kegworth station with what appears to be one such working, via Melton Mowbray and Peterborough. An Italian 40-ton ferry van leads the rake followed by a 12-ton SOV pipe wagon. Further back, a loaded wheel-less 16-ton mineral wagon is hitching a ride on a plate wagon A 50-ton Sturgeon 50-ton bogie rail wagon is prominent towards the centre. The station, a couple of miles south of Ratcliffe-on-Soar, closed on 4th March 1968. The 2½ miles-long 'Kingston-on-Soar Gypsum Mines Railway', dismantled in 1971, ran north from here on the west side, descending sharply before passing under the main lines as it headed east.

Saturday 16th February 1985. Sutton Bonington: The 1150 Ratcliffe-on-Soar to Fletton fly ash train was a personal favourite, not least because timekeeping was generally good. 56067 has just passed under the splendid arch over the four tracks of the Midland Main Line, a mile or so further towards Loughborough. BR built the bespoke wagons in the 1960s, being an adaptation of the 1950s Prestflo cement hopper design. They had a capacity of 22 tons.

Sunday 3rd April 1983. Loughborough: Now in the 'Leicester Gap', 45120 arrives with the 1135 Derby to St Pancras. An example of the somewhat less common yellow ground signal is seen here. These could be passed when 'on', as interlocking would ensure the points in this instance would always be set to the sidings. The signal box, goods warehouse and loading gauge, albeit incomplete, create a traditional railway scene.

Sunday 8th May 1983. Loughborough: 45150 heads powerfully towards its Derby destination with the 1610 departure from St Pancras. The section of line between Loughborough and Syston South Junction (inclusive) was brought within Leicester Signalling Centre's control in the second, of three commissioning phases, on 11th April 1987. The town once had a third station in addition to those on the former Great Central and Midland lines. This was Loughborough (Derby Road) at the end of a LNWR branch, via Shepshed, from Coalville. From there southwards the line was jointly owned with the MR, to connections with both systems at Nuneaton. The LMSR closed it to passengers in April 1931 and closure to freight by BR progressed in stages from November 1955.

Friday 21st January 1977. Loughborough: 20165 heading a mixed fitted northbound freight provides the relatively unusual sight of a single English Electric Type 1 out on the main line. The long train, lead by a 13-ton open wagon and some bogie bolsters, extends back under two bridges. The first carries Nottingham Road and beyond that is the former Great Central Railway's London extension. BR subsequently removed the latter but site works to unite the two preserved sections of the Great Central, which require a new section of embankment as well as a replacement bridge, commenced in early 2016. The bridge beams were put in place on 3rd September 2017.

(*opposite page lower*) **Monday 23rd April 1984. Loughborough**: 56064 passes Loughborough, not quite unnoticed, on the Up goods line with the 1150 Ratcliffe-on-Soar to Fletton fly ash. Though the Class 56 shows clear signs of a Brush Type 4 (Class 47) ancestry, none of the class was built at Loughborough. The first 30 were constructed in Rumania and the remainder at BREL Doncaster. The Station has since gained a third platform on what is now designated the Up and Down slow line. This was initially utilised by 'Ivanhoe' local trains to and from Leicester. The stopping service has since been extended to Lincoln.

(*right*) **Saturday 27th May 1978. Sileby**: A pair of Class 20s, fronted by 20188 head a freight northwards on the Down goods. The station here had closed on 4th March 1968 but was reopened on 27th May 1994, together with Syston and Barrow-on-Soar, as a preliminary phase of the unfulfilled 'Ivanhoe' project for the reinstatement of local services that would have principally included restoration of passenger services between Leicester and Burton-on-Trent line via Coalville and Ashby-de-la-Zouch. Willington, between Burton-on-Trent and Derby, also re-opened as part of this scheme.

(*below*) **Friday 12th May 1978. Sileby**: An unidentified Class 45 passes the signal box with the 1510 Nottingham to St Pancras. This box latterly controlled the sidings about a mile to the north, serving the nearby Mountsorrel stone quarry, which still generates considerable traffic for the railway. The former goods lines were re-designated as slow lines when the 'Ivanhoe' service was introduced as, unlike the originals, all the platforms of the new stations were situated away from the fast lines.

Sunday 11th May 1980. Syston North Junction: 45118 THE ROYAL ARTILLERYMAN heads the 1510 St Pancras to Nottingham past the triangular junction. The impressive signals here gave the option to use the north curve to Syston East Junction. Trains from the Up fast were also able to cross to what was at that time the Up goods, now Up slow.

Sunday 10th February 1985. Syston North Junction: 47443 passes the signal box with the 1540 Derby to St Pancras while crossing over the Fosse Way, former A46. Some of the signals prominent in the previous photo are just visible through the bare trees. The once common overall painted adverts on bridges were often long standing and tended to give an individual character to each structure.

Sunday 11th May 1980. **Syston South Junction**: Most of the passengers on this train, headed by 45133, the 1043 Leeds to St Pancras were no doubt oblivious to the fact that they were on relatively rare metals - the Up goods line. The box controlled the connection with the singled south curve to Syston East Junction and worked that junction from May 1973 after the closure of the box there. The link with the fast lines had been simplified by the installation of a single lead, so favoured by BR, but now in many cases (including here) found to be significantly restricting line capacity. The new Syston station, situated just south of the junction, has just a single platform, as there is only a single, bi-directional slow line between Syston South Junction and Leicester.

Sunday 11th June 1978. **Frisby**: Situated six miles from Syston, heading towards Melton Mowbray, we have a traditional crossing scene of gates, box, cottage and signs. The box, still at the time named 'Frisby Station', is from 1941 and thus of LMSR origin. It still survives, but eventually the line east of here towards Peterborough will be incorporated within the East Midlands Control Centre's area. The MR's line between Syston and Peterborough had opened throughout in 1848, adopting a winding route to serve as many towns and villages as possible.

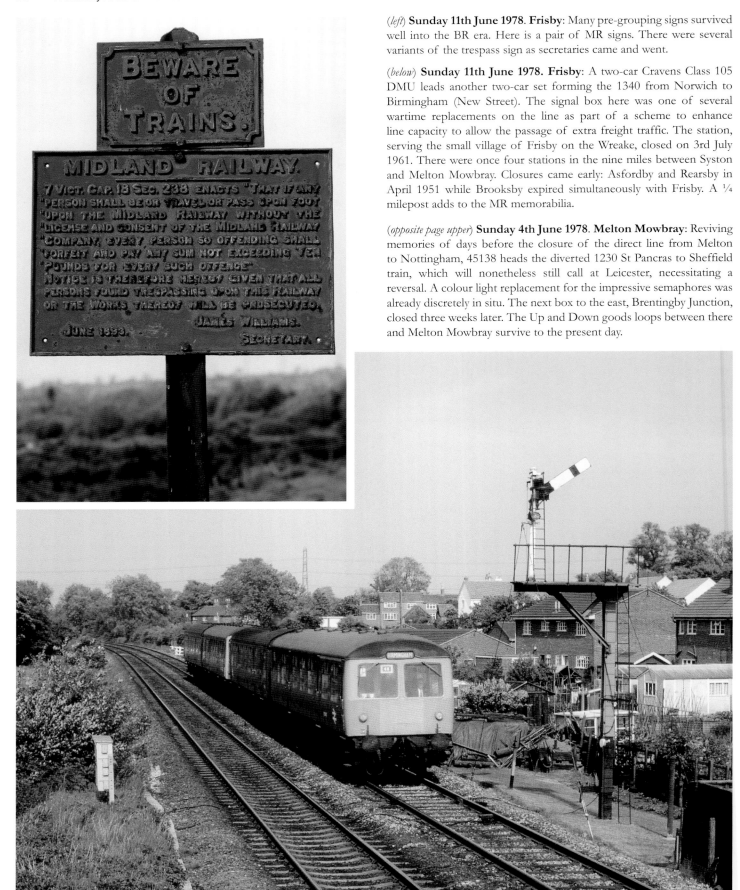

(*left*) **Sunday 11th June 1978**. **Frisby**: Many pre-grouping signs survived well into the BR era. Here is a pair of MR signs. There were several variants of the trespass sign as secretaries came and went.

(*below*) **Sunday 11th June 1978. Frisby**: A two-car Cravens Class 105 DMU leads another two-car set forming the 1340 from Norwich to Birmingham (New Street). The signal box here was one of several wartime replacements on the line as part of a scheme to enhance line capacity to allow the passage of extra freight traffic. The station, serving the small village of Frisby on the Wreake, closed on 3rd July 1961. There were once four stations in the nine miles between Syston and Melton Mowbray. Closures came early: Asfordby and Rearsby in April 1951 while Brooksby expired simultaneously with Frisby. A ¼ milepost adds to the MR memorabilia.

(*opposite page upper*) **Sunday 4th June 1978**. **Melton Mowbray**: Reviving memories of days before the closure of the direct line from Melton to Nottingham, 45138 heads the diverted 1230 St Pancras to Sheffield train, which will nonetheless still call at Leicester, necessitating a reversal. A colour light replacement for the impressive semaphores was already discretely in situ. The next box to the east, Brentingby Junction, closed three weeks later. The Up and Down goods loops between there and Melton Mowbray survive to the present day.

Sunday 4th June 1978. Melton Mowbray: 45124 is captured between the traditional Midland Railway canopies working the diverted 1046 Leeds to St Pancras. Sunday diversions were quite a regular feature, but such services ran nonstop between Leicester and Kettering. The station carried the suffix 'Town' for a while, to distinguish it from the former GN and LNWR Joint line station, which was known as Melton Mowbray (North), situated a half mile across town. It lost its regular passenger service in December 1953, though seasonal trains to Skegness and Mablethorpe, originating at Leicester (Belgrave Road), lasted until 1962, two years prior to total closure.

(*left*) **Sunday 11th June 1978. Melton Mowbray**: The Dalby Road overbridge forms a convenient vantage point for the west end of the station as the 1230 St Pancras to Sheffield is seen again, hauled by an unidentified Class 45. The line to Nottingham diverged at Melton Junction about half a mile to the west of the station. Though severed at the Nottingham end in October 1968, after the withdrawal of the last through freight trains, most of the 17¼ miles of line survives as a test track and various operators have used it over the years. The deliberate destruction of 46009 when colliding with an undamaged nuclear flask on 17th July 1984 is undoubtedly its most famous moment. The very southern end of the line was also utilised to take coal from the new mine at Asfordby, but this closed in 1997 due to geological problems, after barely two years of full production.

(*below*) **Sunday 4th June 1978. Melton Mowbray**: More usual fare in the form the 1246 Birmingham (New Street) to Norwich is arriving behind 31206. The elevated signal box is another of LMSR design, from 1942. Coincidentally, the rival GN and LNWR station was also overseen by an elevated signal box, of LNWR design.

Saturday 18th May 1985. Saxby: 31417 and 31459 are the booked double-header for the strengthened ten-coach Saturday working of the 1020 Birmingham (New Street) to Yarmouth. The train is on the alignment the MR originally intended for this route. However, the land owner Lord Harborough, vigorously refused access to his estate for this to be surveyed and so, instead, the alternative line kept straight on, to the right in this view, before then taking a very sharp curve to achieve the required 90 degrees turn. This became known as 'Lord Harborough's Curve'. Finally, in 1892, a more reasonable successor allowed the railway to be sited as intended and the infamous curve was abandoned. The four-platform station here closed on 6th February 1961. Originally titled 'Saxby West Junction', the signal box once controlled the link to the Midland and Great Northern Joint line to East Anglia. This commenced at an end-on junction at Little Bytham, 13 miles away.

Tuesday 27th October 1981. Oakham: An unidentified pair of Class 20s with a southbound freight passes the Midland Railway's signal box, now Grade II listed, which was immortalised when Airfix chose it as the prototype for a model in the 1950s. The line lost is expresses from St Pancras to the north with the closure of the Melton Mowbray to Nottingham line, the northern extremity of the route from Glendon South Junction. However, recently some of these services have again been routed this way using the east to north curve at Syston.

Tuesday 27th October 1981. **Oakham**: The reverse view: 25307, framed by the Midland Railway footbridge, approaches with a rake of PCA 52-ton cement hoppers from Ketton on the Manton Junction to Peterborough line. Up and Down goods loops remain to the north of the station. Oakham is the county town of Rutland - England's smallest historic county. This visit was, however, during a 23-year period when it was part of Leicestershire.

Monday 18th March 1985. **Gunthorpe**: 31415 attacks the 1 in 143 climb away from Manton Tunnel with the 1332 Norwich to Birmingham (New Street). The colour light splitting distant, for Manton Junction, was not unique but not particularly common. The lenses were carefully positioned so that the lower speed diverging route to the left, towards Peterborough, was clearly indicated.

Tuesday 28th May 1985. **Manton Tunnel**: As with the distant signal, a left-hand green light, at the end of the tunnel indicates that 47050 is set to head its train of 45-ton Monoblock tanks towards Peterborough. Later, the junction at Manton was altered so that trains continuing towards Corby, now designated the 'branch' used the Down line through the tunnel, having crossed over just prior to the tunnel. Recently a conventional junction at Manton has been restored and the crossover removed. The Corby line however, retains its 'branch' designation and is now the lower speed route through the junction.

Thursday 14th February 1985. **Manton Junction**: 25269 slowly leaves the Peterborough line with a parcels train. A four-platform station here, serving both routes had closed on 6th June 1966. There were once east and south boxes but these closed in 1933 and 1958 respectively. Manton Junction box dates from 1913 and still survives. However, BR replaced the mechanical frame with a panel in 1988.

(*previous page lower*) **Thursday 14th February 1985**. **Manton Junction**: 58008 is cautiously taking the Peterborough line as it emerges into a wintry landscape from the 749 yards-long tunnel with the 1150 Ratcliffe-on-Soar to Fletton flash. In 1879, the MR created the junction when it opened the line to Glendon South Junction, just north of Kettering. This was simultaneous with the opening of the Melton Mowbray to Nottingham line, so creating a 49 mile-long alternative route to the north.

(above) **Friday 31st May 1985. Manton Junction**: The signalman here was friendly and an invitation for an unsolicited unofficial box visit was readily accepted. This is the signalman's view as 31271 emerges from the tunnel with another ballast train, this time heading towards Peterborough. Three types of hopper are visible: 24-ton Dogfish, 18-ton Catfish and a 40-ton Sealion.

(right) **Friday 31st May 1985. Manton Junction**: Viewed from above the tunnel, 58019 is observing the severe speed restriction then in force as it negotiates the junction with the 1535 Fletton to Ratcliffe-on-Soar fly ash empties.

(opposite lower) **Friday 31st May 1985. Manton Junction**: 31122 heads past with a train of Sealion ballast hoppers from Loughborough to Bedford. Even after the closure of the line north of Melton Mowbray, the truncated route, from Syston to Glendon South Junction, was ideally placed to allow freights to be kept away from the line via Leicester, and its various restrictive two-track sections. After the closure of the south box, Manton Junction was given an Intermediate Block Section (IBS) on the Up line towards Corby. 31122 is passing the outer IBS distant, 1048 yards from the IBS home. There was also an IBS on the Down line, to reduce the length of the block section to Oakham.

Friday 16th October 1981. **Ketton**: 25067 passes with the 1015 Birmingham (New Street) to Norwich. The Midland Railway home signal on the Down line is a notable survivor though unfortunately not particularly well sited for photography! This is the site of Ketton and Collyweston station, which closed on 6th June 1966.

Friday 16th October 1981. **Stamford**: We stray briefly into Lincolnshire. Just 3¼ miles along the line from Ketton, 31279 arrives from the west with a rake of 20-ton Prestflo cement wagons. A prominent landowner objected to the GNR building its 'towns line' from Peterborough to Doncaster through the town, it already being served by the MR. Fortunately this was not one of the cross-country routes culled in the Beeching era and thus the substantial town continues to enjoy a station on the network, but not on the East Coast Main Line!

Friday 16th October 1981. Stamford: Did he catch it? No time to spare as 'skinhead' 31418 arrives with the 0939 Norwich to Birmingham (New Street). After the local opposition had abated, the Great Northern Railway did build a station in Stamford, at Water Street. This was the terminus of branches from Essendine on the ECML and Wansford on the LNWR's line between Northampton and Peterborough. The branch to Wansford closed completely in 1931. For just over two years prior to closure of the Essendine branch in June 1959, BR had diverted trains to the former MR station via a pre-existing connection between the adjoining parallel lines. For a while, to avoid confusion, the former MR station had the suffix 'Town' and its GNR counterpart 'East'. (*below*) Here on the same day we have a glimpse of the extremely attractive town in the background. The signal box is nice too! Meanwhile, 31279, having detached from the cement wagons, is busy with some shunting in the coal yard. After closure of the yard in May 1983, the signal box passed into private ownership and was moved a little closer to the station.

Friday 13th May 1983. Leicester: Having travelled via Stamford and Melton Mowbray, 31419 is clearly being routed into Platform 4 on arrival with a cross-country service, the 1133 Norwich to Birmingham (New Street). BR built the Leicester Signalling Centre on the east side of the line just north of the station. The immediate Leicester area and the line as far south as Little Bowden Junction, Market Harborough formed the first phase of the demise of 'The Leicester Gap' with the manual signal boxes closing on 29th June 1986. Leicester Signalling Centre closed on 31st December 2011: the area then coming under the East Midlands Control Centre. (*below*) Later, 37059 arrives with empty coaching stock. Bell Lane signal box, 600 yards to the north is visible beyond Leicester North. By this time, the next box north of there was Syston South Junction, Humberstone Road Junction having closed in September 1979. Leicester Depot partly seen on the right, then a hive of activity, now lies derelict. Various goods stations were at one time located north of here, mainly on the west side. One of these was built by the LNWR, which had running powers over parts of the MR.. A number of sidings serving private premises added to the complexity of lines, which extended for a mile.

Friday 13th May 1983. **Leicester**: 25133 heads a rake of engineer's stock Sealion ballast hoppers along the Down main. The canopies were recent, the station having lost its overall roof in the 1970s. It previously had the suffix 'London Road' but this became superfluous when Leicester (Central) on the Great Central's London extension closed in 1969. Leicester also once had two termini: the previously mentioned GNR's at Belgrave Road and West Bridge at the end of the 1832-built Leicester and Swannington Railway. This line tapped the rich Leicestershire coalfield to the west and subsequently became part of the MR. West Bridge, where the basic facilities were in total contrast to those at Belgrave Road, closed to passengers in September 1928, but freight traffic lingered until April 1966. (*below*) 45111 GRENADIER GUARDSMAN emerges into a brief patch of sunlight with the 1230 St Pancras to Sheffield. The banner repeaters were necessary due to the extremely poor sighting for the semaphores situated just beyond the bridge. Like many stations of a comparable size, Leicester was once busy-enough to need one or more signal boxes within the station buildings in the centre of the station to supervise movements to and from adjacent trailing connections as well as the passage of trains along the platform lines, which were split into two sections. The decline in traffic, coupled with changed methods of working brought about their obsolescence. The boxes, Leicester Station East and Leicester Station West closed in June 1970. However, thoughts are now turning to increasing the station's capacity.

Sunday 11th May 1980. **Leicester**: 47536 passes London Road Junction signal box with the 0945 Manchester (Piccadilly) to St Pancras. This box, of LMSR design, replaced the original, destroyed in a collision between two trains in December 1935. Leicester's imposing station building dates from 1892 and clearly provided the inspiration for Nottingham, 12 years later. Up and Down goods lines, which avoided the station are on the right. The distant signal is for Leicester North. Of particular interest are the Up signals for the four platform lines, which in addition to being provided with banner repeaters, also had short arms to aid visibility.

(*opposite upper*) **Friday 13th May 1983**. **Leicester**: 45131 waits for departure time at Platform 2 with the 1525 St Pancras to Sheffield. Bell Lane had yet to accept this train. From the start of the following week, BR introduced a further tranche of HSTs on Midland Main Line services, virtually, but not quite, eliminating all locomotive-hauled workings. Prior to December 1968, there was a signal box between Leicester North and Bell Lane. This was Leicester Engine Shed Sidings, situated on the Up side. This controlled and protected a trailing crossover running between two flanking sidings, which had connections to all four main lines.

Sunday 29th April 1984. Leicester: 45106 has just passed the site of Cattle Market Sidings with the 1700 Derby St Pancras. This is the view from the overbridge carrying Welford Road, on the approach to Knighton Tunnel, just under a mile south of the station. A signal box here closed in April 1969. Nevertheless, London Road Junction's Down goods distant still provided some signalling interest.

Sunday 29th April 1984. Leicester: Welford Road bridge still carried a Midland Railway STICK NO BILLS sign. (*below*) 31170 working the 1640 Birmingham (New Street) to Norwich has just emerged from the 104 yards-long Knighton Tunnel and is passing the site of the ticket platform at Welford Road, which was also used for alighting purposes on market days by a few LNWR trains from the Nuneaton line. The parallel two yards-longer tunnel housing the goods lines became disused in the track rationalisation programme when BR re-signalled the area in 1986. However, the track bed remains tantalisingly vacant should the need for increased line capacity ever make reinstatement desirable, something that is looking increasingly likely.

(*left*) **Monday 18th March 1985**. **Coalville**: 56085 is seen heading east past the site of Coalville (Town) station and an imposing signal box, in the town centre. Upon closure, the box was moved to the nearby Snibston Discovery Park, sadly now closed. The adjacent box at Mantle Lane now remotely controls the crossing. Now situated 16½ miles by rail west of Leicester, Coalville was the eponymous centre of the Leicestershire coalfield. It is just over a mile to the east of Swannington. It had a once-busy depot, which however closed in 1990. Having lost its passenger trains on 7th September 1964, at one time it seemed the line would emulate the Robin Hood line in having a restored passenger service taking over as coal traffic disappeared. As we have seen, some stations north of Leicester were re-opened as a preliminary phase of the so-called 'Ivanhoe Line' project.

(*below*) **Monday 18th March 1985**. **Bardon Hill**: 56085 is seen again, at Bardon Hill 1½ miles west of Coalville, with 51-ton PGA hoppers in Tarmac livery. This is the railhead for one of the two quarries on the line; stone being the only source of traffic on the branch, the western end of which now sees very little activity. It could have been so very different had the plan to restore the passenger service come to fruition. The undulating nature of the line, partly due to historic mining subsidence, is readily apparent in this view.

Monday 18th March 1985. **Bardon Hill**: 56085 passes the happily still open signal box. The MR built this in 1899. It now has electrical switches rather than a mechanical lever frame. It is estimated that the nearby quarry has sufficient reserves to last for most of this century. The LNWR's line from Loughborough (Derby Road), having first served Coalville with its own station 'East', passed under the MR about three-quarters of a mile west of here. There was a west to south connecting spur from the MR; it was from the junction southwards that the line became LNWR and MR joint. (*below*) 58016 had travelled over the mainly single line from Knighton South Junction on the Midland Main Line as it approached with MGR empties. This locomotive resides in preservation at the Barrow Hill Roundhouse Railway Centre. The Midland Railway opened the seven miles line from Knighton, south of Leicester, to Desford on the Leicester and Swannington Railway in 1849, so bypassing the notoriously restricted single-track Glenfield Tunnel on what became known as the West Bridge branch. Simultaneously, it extended the line westwards, creating a 29 miles-long through route to a triangular junction with the Derby to Birmingham line, just south of Burton-on-Trent.

(*right*) **Sunday 29th April 1984**. **Knighton South Junction**: The 0858 Leeds to St Pancras HST heads past the LMSR box, which dated from 1936. This was by now the only connection with the line to Coalville and Burton-on-Trent. Knighton North Junction, which once controlled a north to west curve, had closed in May 1968. A single Up and Down goods line now suffices between here and Wigston North Junction, 1½ miles to the south.

(*below*) **Sunday 29th April 1984**. **Wigston North Junction**: Consecutively numbered Class 47s, 47420 and 47419 pass the box with the 1305 Nottingham to St Pancras. The line on the left is the former LNWR western side of a triangle, the next box being Glen Parva Junction. Prior to 1st January 1962, trains could also continue due south from here on the original Midland Counties Railway to Rugby. This provided a link to London (Euston) using trains of the London and Birmingham Railway, forerunner of the LNWR. However, the MR chose this place to commence its own route towards London, initially via Bedford to Hitchin and thence over the GNR to King's Cross. This opened in 1857, but the shared section soon became very congested. An independent line to London was clearly required for all the freight, as well passenger traffic. Thus, in 1868 the MR opened its own line south of Bedford to London, providing extensive freight-handling facilities near St Pancras station. Consequently, the Rugby line became a branch, serving very little purpose. Usually, it is the earliest lines that have survived, but this was an exception.

Thursday 15th May 1980. Wigston South Junction: 45122 with the 0758 Leeds to St Pancras has exactly 95½ miles left of its journey as it encounters the first of many severe curves south of Leicester. The chord, linking with the Nuneaton line that forms the base of a triangle, is visible on the left hand side. The Rugby line crossed it on the level. Wigston (Magna) station was situated just south of the bridge from where this photo was taken. It closed on 1st January 1968. There were two other stations in the vicinity, Wigston (South) on the Rugby route, which perished with the line's closure and the third, Wigston (Glen Parva) on the LNWR's Nuneaton line, which also closed in 1968. However a replacement for that, situated just a little way further east, named 'South Wigston', opened in 1986. (*below*) 25114 approaches with a south bound freight. The rake is very mixed with a couple of 13-ton opens, several 16-ton minerals wagons, a Presflo covered hopper, a fitted van followed by a small capacity tank, and a continental ferry van. Signals offering the choice of a divergence onto the Down goods line are visible in the distance. This was once a busy location, also having many sidings on the Up side of the line. There was also an engine shed. The LMSR closed this in 1935, but the site was eventually utilised for wagon repairs, which lasted until the 1970s.

Sunday 29th April 1984. **Kilby Bridge**: The 1450 Derby to St Pancras HST passes the distinctive signal box, 1½ miles east of Wigston South Junction. This subsequently found a new home at Hammersmith, the western end of the Midland Railway-Butterley's line in Derbyshire. To the west of here were Up and Down goods lines. Following track simplification during the 1980s resignalling scheme, this is now the location of the junction with the Nuneaton line for trains to and from the south.

Thursday 15th May 1980. **Kibworth**: Hauling the 1100 from Sheffield to St Pancras, 45116 has reached the summit after an almost unrelenting 30 miles climb from Trent, albeit gradually until Wigston, and is passing the termination of the Up goods line. Until 1968, Kibworth North box was situated here, but extending the area of control of Kibworth signal box, just three-quarters of a mile to the east was an obvious economy. Some signals belonging to Wistow, only a mile to the north, are visible in the distance.

Thursday 12th May 1983. **Market Harborough**: 45140 with the 1425 Nottingham to St Pancras, cautiously approaches the station area. Visible on the left is the disused, former LNWR Rugby/Northampton to Peterborough line, which the train has crossed over a minute or so previously. A couple of miles north of here on that line was Welham Junction, where the GN and LNW Joint line diverged. This provided a route that eventually led, via Melton Mowbray, to Newark, the surviving part of which we saw earlier in the journey.

Thursday 12th May 1983. **Market Harborough**: 45143 5TH ROYAL INNISKILLING DRAGOON GUARDS is 83 miles into its journey heading the 1405 St Pancras to Nottingham. The LNWR reached here in 1845 and the Midland Railway in its quest for its own line to London, upon arrival in 1857, at first shared a two-platform station and just over a mile of line. In the 1880s, the MR built a bridge over the LNWR on the site of the former junction to the north and laid its own, parallel line, with separate platforms on the east side of the LNWR. Connections between the two railways were minimal, being via a set of exchange sidings just north of the station. In 1924, just after both companies had been absorbed into the LMSR, a full junction, here now only partially extant, was installed to enable through running to and from the ex LNWR lines south of Market Harborough.

Thursday 12th May 1983. **Market Harborough**: The 1510 Nottingham to St Pancras HST sweeps around the severe curve. At its zenith, the station boasted four through platforms and additionally on the LNWR side, a bay for each direction. BR withdrew the passenger service to Northampton (Castle) in January 1960, though it subsequently reinstated a limited service. A major decline in services at the station followed on 6th June 1966 with the withdrawal of passenger trains between Rugby and Peterborough. After the closure of the last of the two former Midland Railway boxes here in 1968, a former LNWR box, later designated 'No. 3', assumed full control of the immediate station area until the opening of Leicester Signalling Centre in 1986. (*below*) 47364 negotiates the similarly sharp bend from the south with an unfitted freight. Little Bowden Junction's distant is below the home signal. The signal was positioned on the Down side to aid visibility. The line to the left of the Up line was the connection to the MR's once quite extensive goods facilities just to the east of the station. The LNWR had corresponding facilities to the west of the station together with a small engine shed, which lasted until 1965.

Thursday 12th May 1983. Market Harborough: The 1500 St Pancras to Nottingham HST enters the station. BR had sited the replacement station buildings to facilitate easing the reverse curves in the area, but this is still yet to happen. However, current indications are that the work will proceed in the near future. The rails of the last remnant of the LNWR system, the branch to Northampton, await only the track lifting train. After two prior closures and reopenings, it had finally closed to passenger traffic in August 1973, but lingered on until August 1981, mainly for overnight parcels trains. A 1½ miles section survives as the Northampton and Lamport Railway.

Thursday 12th May 1983. Little Bowden Junction: 45125, running under clear signals, eases round the curve with the 1230 St Pancras to Sheffield. Situated half a mile south of Market Harborough station, the signal box, previously at the start of an Up goods line was still an important block post and oversaw a foot crossing.

Thursday 15th May 1980. **Desborough**: 25114, seen earlier in the day at Wigston South Junction, is captured again, in Northamptonshire, returning northwards. The unfitted consist is lead by a General Utility Van, followed by a 45-ton tank and some long wheelbase vans. A pair of 21-ton hoppers brings up the rear. Fire destroyed Desborough North box, seen in the distance, in March 1981, bringing about the demise of the Up goods line from Little Bowden Junction. This was the summit of approximately 1 in 130 ascents from both directions. The nearby station, called Desborough and Rothwell, was another 1st January 1968 victim.

Friday 3rd September 1982. **Glendon North Junction**: 45130 rounds another curve with the 1300 Nottingham to St Pancras. Since the loss of Desborough North, the block section to the west, to Little Bowden Junction was an operationally challenging 7½ miles. This was the point where the 75 miles-long four-track railway, all the way to London, commenced. This was the longest section of continuous quadruple line in the country. The final phase of the implementation of control by Leicester Signalling Centre saw the closure of the signal boxes from here to Irchester South on 5th December 1987.

Friday 3rd September 1982. **Glendon South Junction**: 45077 and 45065 approach the junction, on the line from Corby with a rake of 51-ton PGA hoppers en route from Mountsorrel to Radlett Redland Stone Terminal. The retaining wall almost totally hides the Down slow. (*below*) Glendon South Junction: 47451 heads past on the Up main with the 1400 Sheffield to St Pancras. The following month HSTs took over about half of the services on the Midland Main Line. Glendon South Junction signal box, half a mile south of Glendon North Junction, closed in 1973 - the junction being worked from then onwards by its former near neighbour. Glendon South Junction did not control the now designated 'main lines'. However, prior to the closure of the Melton Mowbray to Nottingham route in the 1960s, the lines to the right, though designated as 'slow lines', also handled express passenger trains.

Friday 3rd September 1982. Glendon South Junction: 25250 leaves the town of Kettering behind at it heads along the Down slow line on an impressive looking stretch of railway with a 'Fletliner', bringing bricks from the London Brick Company's terminal at Stewartby, Bedfordshire to Garston, near Liverpool. Each wagon could take three flats, each loaded to 15 tons. Trains were made up in sets of five wagons. The formation along here is now three tracks, including a bi-directional slow line.

Friday 4th April 1980. Kettering: 25320 approaches on the Up slow with a short mixed fitted freight. In the consist are a 21-ton end-door open, a 45-ton Monoblock tank and 16-ton mineral wagons. Kettering engine shed had been situated immediately to the east of this viewpoint. Kettering North signal box, which controlled its connections to the main lines, closed in 1967, leaving signalling of the station under the supervision of just one box.

(*above*) **Friday 4th April 1980. Kettering**: A gleaming 'Peak' 45068 eases through the impressive station with an unidentified train to the south, probably a Good Friday extra. Not surprisingly, the whole station has Grade II listed status. The MR expanded the station to four platforms in 1879 as part of the line-quadrupling programme that it completed five years later. Kettering, a town once noted for the manufacture of boots and shoes, was only served by the MR. There was a full range of goods facilities on the southeast side of the station.

(*left*) **Friday 4th April 1980. Kettering**: Midland Railway railwayana is on view, in the form of a zero milepost and gradient sign. The milepost referred to the trailing Down side junction with the branch to Cransley and Loddington at this location. Had it been a facing junction, the mileage measured from London would have continued along the branch. The MR built this to serve an iron works at Cransley, two miles to the west, later extending it by a similar distance to an iron ore quarry at Loddington. The latter closed in 1970 but the iron works site was later taken over by the firm of George Cohen, which scrapped many locomotives in the 1960 and 1970s.

Sunday 23rd May 1982. Kettering: 45064 is heading north on the Down slow line with the 0900 St Pancras to Sheffield, to be diverted via Corby and Melton Mowbray. After some track rationalisation at the north end of the station, there was no further link between fast and slow lines prior to the divergence of the routes at Glendon South Junction; hence the relatively unusually appearance, at that time, of a passenger train on these rails.

Friday 4th April 1980. Kettering: 45132 is arriving with the 1509 St Pancras to Nottingham. The signal box, Kettering Station, like Kilby Bridge, found a new home at the Midland Railway-Butterley, at Swanwick Junction. The box from Ais Gill lies between them! The telegraph poles and yard lamps add to the railway atmosphere, though ominously, all the sidings are empty. The Cransley branch is the line diverging to the right in the foreground. At one time, some of the sidings had been used to store locomotives awaiting the one-way journey to Cohen's scrap yard. The branch closed just a few months after the date of this photo, on 1st October 1980.

Friday 3rd September 1982. Kettering Junction: Viewed from Pytchley Road overbridge, 31315 is signalled to continue on the Up slow in the late afternoon with a Toton to Acton freight. To the front of the rake is a mixture of 16 and 21-ton coal wagons. By 1982, almost 20 years after the Beeching report and the rapid expansion of the motorway network, such freights containing yard-sorted single or small sets of wagons for individual customers were something of an anachronism. Kettering South signal box, between here and the station 1¼ miles to the north, had been another 1967 casualty. (*below*) 45046 ROYAL FUSILIER passes with the 1705 St Pancras to Derby. This was formerly the junction with the Midland Railway's branch to Huntingdon, which lost its passenger service in June 1959. Much later, this location was the commencement of a pared two-track section of railway towards Wellingborough, but due to the need for extra line capacity, a bi-directional slow line has now been reinstated. The restoration of the fourth track is proposed as part of the Bedford to Corby electrification scheme.

Friday 22nd August 1980. **Wellingborough**: Viewed from the Mill Road overbridge, 56061 heads south on the Up goods with the afternoon Mountsorrel Redlands stone train, seen earlier on a different occasion at Glendon South Junction. Wellingborough North signal box, closed in December 1962, was on the Up side, near to the rear of the train. However, Finedon Road signal box is just visible: framed by one of the arches carrying its namesake road over the railway. Nearer to the camera, the finial on the former Midland Railway post of its distant is at rather a crooked angle!

Thursday 7th May 1987. **Wellingborough**: Seven years later and the same location has 58007 with a loaded southbound MGR, perpetuating one of the principal original functions of this line. The train is from Toton, bound for Northfleet cement works, in Kent and is departing after a crew change. Wellingborough, being 65 miles from London, was an ideal place to act as an important 'half-way' for freight traffic from the East Midlands to London. It had extensive marshalling yards and a depot, best known as 15A. The facilities also included a hostel for enginemen. Part of the shed still survives as a Grade II listed building.

Friday 22nd August 1980. Wellingborough: 45107 passes Finedon Road signal box, three-quarters of a mile north of the station, hauling the 1300 Sheffield to St Pancras. The marshalling yard in the background, which once dealt with the staple product of the area, iron ore, still has an air of prosperity. Neilsons Sidings signal box controlled the northern end of this. In its heyday, Finedon Road would have been very busy, since as well as controlling connections to the engine shed, there was a link to Wellingborough Ironworks, which was immediately to the west of the line at this point. The works closed in 1962.

Friday 22nd August 1980. **Wellingborough**: One of the high arches of Mill Road bridge frames ex works 45045 COLDSTREAM GUARDSMAN, arriving with the terminating 1012 parcels from Nottingham, just as 45130 commences the opposite journey with the 1108 from St Pancras. The signal box dated from 1893, being extended in 1915. The station was the terminus for local services from Northampton and the nearby Higham Ferrers branch. These ceased in May 1964 and June 1959 respectively. In addition to having platforms on each of the four lines, the station also had a south-facing bay. The slow line platforms went out of regular use in 1959, but the short platform forming the east side of the island serving the Up main, is retained on the current single Up and Down slow line. (*below*) The signaller at Finedon Road has yet to clear the signals for a northbound train. The barrow crossing's warning indicator, interlocked with a combination of track circuits and the Up and Down home signals, shows TRAIN COMING. Finedon Road's Down goods line distant was later relocated to below the right-hand home signal. Whereas the stations we have seen at Chesterfield, Derby, Loughborough and Nottingham once had the suffix 'Midland' to distinguish them from the station formerly of the other company serving the same place, Wellingborough had the suffix 'Midland Road', an LMSR naming, neatly combining the names of nearest thoroughfare and original owning company!

Friday 22nd August 1980. Wellingborough: Mill Road again provides the vantage point, this time for the sight of 25266 and 25316 with the 'Fletliner' from Stewartby to Garston. The LMSR-built 1940s Wellingborough Junction signal box, to the south of the station, was switched out, pending formal closure. The junction was with a chord to the closed former LNWR line linking Northampton to Peterborough on which Wellingborough's other station, 'London Road', was situated. The severe curve at the south end of the station was the last of the many such curves south of Leicester, which together prevent sustained high speed running. The engineering of this section of line, built in austere times principally with coal traffic in mind, is in sharp contrast to the large-radius curves and gradual gradients on the original Midland Counties Railway's route between Trent and Rugby.

Thursday 7th May 1987. **Wellingborough**: Once again, changes are readily apparent after a seven-year interval: Wellingborough Junction signal box, which formally closed in November 1983, having been demolished. 47313 is seen with a northbound train of empty 100-ton tankers designated for petrol, believed to be from Langley, near Slough to Humber Oil Refinery at Immingham, via Trent. By this time the next signal box south of here, Irchester South, was the limit of the 'Leicester Gap' as Sharnbrook had closed in May 1981, thus marginally extending West Hampstead PSB's area of control. (*below*) Just days away from the end of locomotive hauled trains on the Midland Main Line, 45132 accelerates after the station stop for the short seven miles run to another stop, at Kettering with the 1735 St Pancras to Derby. By the end of 1987, the combination of semaphores and 'Peaks' on the Midland Main Line would be but a memory.

Sunday 2nd January 1977. Rectory Junction: A Birmingham Railway Carriage & Wagon Company Class 104 DMU crosses the River Trent with the 1510 from Grantham to Nottingham.

ACKNOWLEDGEMENTS

David Allen of Book Law Publications.

Steve Waddington of Amadeus.

Hayden Reed, Nick Quinn and Pete Lane - for providing information for some of the captions.

John West for his tuition in Information Technology.

To the late Les Fletcher and all the other railway staff who facilitated enjoyment of the railway along the way.

BIBLIOGRAPHY

An Illustrated History of Leicester's Railways - John Stretton - Irwell Press

An Illustrated History of Mansfield's Railways - Paul Anderson and Jack Cupit - Irwell Press

A Regional History of the Railways of Great Britain, Volume 9 The East Midlands - Robin Leleux - David & Charles

British Rail Layout Plans of the 1950s (various vols) - John Swift - Signalling Record Society

Last Train From Trent Station - Geoffrey Kingscott - Geoffrey Kingscott Consultants Ltd.

Modern Locomotives Illustrated (various vols) - Editor Colin J Marsden - Key Publishing

Passengers No More - G. Daniels and L. Dench - Ian Allan

Rail Centres: Nottingham - Michael A. Vanns - Book Law Publications

Signal Box Register Vol 3 LNER (Southern Area) - Signalling Record Society

Six Bells Junction railtour website.

The Great Northern Railway in the East Midlands (Vols 1-4) - Alfred Henshaw - RCTS

Toton – Early Diesels in the East Midlands - Don Beecroft - Book Law Publications